I0815188

BEYOND *the* LIES

A BOOK FOR THE LOVED ONES OF ADDICTS OR ALCOHOLICS

BEYOND *the* LIES

Addiction is much more than drinking alcohol and using drugs

C.S. JACKSON

Beyond the Lies: Addiction is much more
than drinking alcohol or using drugs

Published by Clovercroft Publishing, Franklin, Tennessee
ClovercroftPublishingGroup.com

Edited by Ann Tatlock

Cover and Interior Layout Design by Suzanne Lawing

Cover Image by Jason Talevi

ISBN: 978-1-968127-03-9 (print)

Printed in the United States of America

Contents

ACKNOWLEDGMENTS

First, thank you to my partner Nicole for sticking with me through my drinking years and for being an active participant in our recovery. Living with me, she had a front-row seat to being a loved one of me, an addict and alcoholic. Her encouragement, support and input were critical to this book. She has allowed me to share her story with the world to help you. Nicole, I am forever grateful that you are my partner in life!

Thank you to my two beautiful children for their positive support, periodically asking me "Dad, how's your book coming?" … for the entire five years it has taken me to bring this to you!

I would like to thank my brother Glenn and his partner Eileen. They both agreed to let me share their stories with you. Eileen made me realize the need for one of us addicts or alcoholics to give people like you, the loved ones, the "secret decoder ring" to our behavior.

Thank you to my editor and coach Julie Hannon for all her wonderful work, providing amazing technical and emotional insight. She helped shape my writing style to really connect with you. Many times, we debated how things should be written and lucky for you, I mostly listened to her!

Christi LeClair has been invaluable in bringing this book to market. She reminded me that even the most powerful story can make an impact only if people know about it—and thanks to her guidance, this one reached you. She also brought editing insights shaped by her own experience as the loved one of generational addicts. This project needed you, so thank you for being there.

My very talented, lifelong friend Jason Talevi gave me his time and creativity to develop the image for the cover. He showed tremendous patience as we worked through multiple different concepts. Thank you, Jason, for being my friend, for your positive support on the entire project, and of course for the awesome book cover image!

Finally, a big thank you to the many people who allowed me to interview them and share their stories in this book. These parents and family members revisited painful memories of their addict and alcoholic loved ones to help you.

CHAPTER 1:

Nicole and Me

Your loved one might be a drug addict or an alcoholic, or both. In this book I will use the term addict-alcoholic to encompass all scenarios. If you have a loved one who is addicted to any substance, be it drugs or alcohol or both, *Beyond the Lies* is for you.

When you live with an addict-alcoholic, it affects you deeply. The effects addiction has on the addict-alcoholic's loved ones, people like you, can differ depending on your relationship to them. You might be a partner to, a parent of, a child of, a sibling of, or a friend of an addict-alcoholic.

- Partners may be chronically manipulated and feel like they are going crazy.
- Parents may have a tremendous sense of guilt that they could not prevent their child from becoming an addict-alcoholic.
- Children of an addicted parent grow up in an emotionally unsafe, tumultuous environment and frequently

carry unhealthy coping mechanisms into their adult relationships.

- Siblings may develop deep resentments toward the addict-alcoholic for taking all the attention and causing so much strife in the family.
- Lifelong friends may have to make the tough decision to cut ties with the addict-alcoholic to distance themselves from the chaos and selfishness of addiction.

Please know that you are not alone! Everybody who has an addict-alcoholic in their life has been affected by it.

I am Craig Jackson, your author and guide through *Beyond the Lies.* My grandfather was an alcoholic who never found sobriety. I grew up with an active alcoholic dad who found sobriety when I was fourteen years old. My oldest brother struggled with addiction for decades, and he is now sober.

The secondhand effects of addiction and alcoholism are as real as the effects of secondhand smoke.

I have experienced the abandonment a child feels when he has grown up with an alcoholic parent. I know what the loneliness feels like as a nine-year-old looking over at the stands during my baseball game and seeing every other kid's parent there but mine, when he promised he would come. *He promised!* I have experienced anxiety and tension as my alcoholic parent got home from work: *Did he have any drinks before coming home? Hopefully he had enough to take the edge off, to be affectionate and playful. Or did he have too many drinks and he's going to be mean?*

I have experienced the anger toward an active addict-alcoholic sibling who repeatedly takes advantage of his parents and breaks their hearts. I know what it's like to feel bad for my nieces and nephews, knowing what they are going through because I had those same experiences in my childhood with my dad.

So, I am the grandson of, a son of, and the brother of addict-alcoholics. The crazy thing about my experiences growing up is that they did not stop me from becoming an addict-alcoholic myself. Addiction kind of runs in our family!

In 2014, I was graced enough to get sober. As I got sober and worked hard at my recovery, I came to realize that living with an addict-alcoholic is, at best, challenging. I know from deep exploration of what I did as an active addict-alcoholic, and from my childhood experiences that loved ones like you become emotionally traumatized from your experience living with an addict-alcoholic.

By nature, addiction is a very selfish disease. Addict-alcoholics will do anything to protect their ability to drink and use drugs. This includes chronically manipulating their loved ones, people like you. The selfishness causes them to be "takers" in their relationships, exploiting your love for them.

I wanted to somehow give back to you, so I wrote this book. My goal is to pull back the curtain on the addict-alcoholic's inner world and their interactions with their loved ones. I want to help you get in touch with the thoughts and feelings you may have from living with an addicted loved one. My hope is that this book will help you in these ways:

- understand why addict-alcoholics use drugs and alcohol the way they do,
- understand the mental and emotional wounds you may have sustained by living with an addict-alcoholic, and
- begin to heal both yourself and your relationship with the addict-alcoholic.

Let's kick things off by sharing the stories of my wife Nicole and me. My side of the story describes what was going on in my head during my drinking and drugging years. Her story describes what she went through being in relationship with me and how my behaviors made her feel. Same relationship, two different perspectives. The two stories will show how, when you are in a relationship with an addict-alcoholic, each person lives in and experiences a different reality.

First my story. Although I am both an alcoholic and addict, in this part of my story I focus on my drinking. Later in this book I will share my stories of using drugs.

* * *

My story about manipulating Nicole:

"My solution to this dilemma was to systematically control Nicole's perception of my drinking."

I never really drank alcohol much before college. When I went to college, I drank like most other students did. I went to parties on the weekends, and as was the case with most everyone at those parties, the goal was to get drunk and have fun. I never really drank during the week, and my drinking certainly did not interfere with my grades as I was on the Dean's list every semester.

College was where Nicole and I met. We were both in the same engineering program and from the instant our paths crossed, we really connected. We started dating in 1994. Nicole and I had many things in common: we were both not your typical engineer, we liked the same music and had the same views on life. We would go to parties together and go see our favorite bands play. We loved being together and could have a great time just mopping the floor!

For about five years our relationship came easily and was very fulfilling and fun. We didn't live together during those first five years and would spend every weekend together. Sometimes I would visit her during the week. At that time, I was starting to drink more. I loved the feeling of being buzzed, but I didn't think my drinking was an issue.

Nicole did not like to drink; she didn't like how it made her feel. She also grew up with a father who abused alcohol, so she had little tolerance for excessive drinking. This meant I didn't have a "drinking buddy" in Nicole. When I was with her, I didn't drink much because I knew she wouldn't like it, so I would just wait until I was back on my own to drink. Little by little, I drank more and more. Eventually I started to use alcohol every day.

At about the five-year mark of our relationship we bought a condominium and moved in together. Now that Nicole and I were together all the time, I knew I had to cut back on my drinking because she would not like it. I thought to myself, I need to grow up and stop drinking so much. In my mind drinking was not a huge problem and I could still control it. So, I tried to cut way back.

Unexpectedly, as I reduced my alcohol consumption, I was unable to fall asleep at night. Thoughts crossed my mind that maybe I couldn't fall asleep because I was becoming dependent on alcohol. The notion horrified me, and I felt some shame. Despite feeling disturbed at those thoughts, my solution to the sleeping problem was to drink at least four beers before going to bed. To accomplish this without Nicole knowing, I stayed up later than she did, drinking after she went to bed. I remember a few times she came downstairs late at night to see why I wasn't in bed yet. When I looked up at her, beer in hand, I felt flush and had a sinking feeling in my stomach because she caught me drinking. I felt ashamed of myself for not being able to cut back.

Over the next few years, my drinking crept into full-blown addiction. When I was stressed, alcohol was the answer to relax. When we were doing something fun, drinking would make it even more fun. When I was sad, alcohol would numb the pain. Alcohol became my only tool for coping with life.

Because I had no way of relaxing without drinking, and Nicole did not like to drink, I was in a tough spot. The thing I needed to do most to cope with life was not acceptable to her. My solution to this dilemma was to systematically try to control Nicole's perception of my drinking.

I became an expert hider. I thought that if Nicole did not see me drinking, she wouldn't know, and more importantly, I wouldn't get called out on it. I drank on my drive home from work. When she went out to do errands, I jumped on the opportunity to drink. If she were around, I would make up reasons to go down to the garage where I could drink from my hidden stashes. I continued to stay up later than Nicole at night so I could drink enough to fall asleep.

I became obsessed; figuring out when I could drink was something I thought about all the time. I reached the point where I drank every day, all day. I developed an elaborate scheme of hiding spots and excuses to enable my constant drinking.

I never consciously thought to myself, "I am going to control Nicole now." If I felt like a situation was going to prevent me from drinking the way I needed to, it caused tremendous fear in me. My fight-or-flight response would kick in, and I felt like I was drowning. Like a drowning person would, I did whatever it took to quell the fear. That included twisting the reality Nicole lived in. Controlling her perception of my drinking became autonomic. Like breathing, I did it without even thinking about it.

Although I thought I was not hurting anybody but myself, our relationship was becoming strained. Being with her and having fun did not come as easily as it used to. We fought a lot more than ever, and a distance grew between us which had never been there before. I did not understand why it was happening, and I blamed her. When we fought, I would tell her that things had become the way they were because of her.

We got married nine years into our relationship, and I hoped getting married would bring us back close again. To my dismay, our relationship continued to feel strained. I had no idea why and it stressed me out. As usual, my solution to the problem was to continue numbing myself with alcohol.

About thirteen years into our relationship, we decided to build a house, and we sold our condominium. While our house was under construction, we moved into a small, two-room apartment. My drinking was as bad as ever. I had to somehow develop a whole new scheme to drink the way I needed to without Nicole knowing. In that apartment, I felt like the walls were closing in on me; I felt the feeling of drowning again.

Without the hiding spots I had in our large condominium, I moved onto different strategies of controlling Nicole's perception of my drinking. One thing I did was keep an open case of beer on top of the refrigerator in her plain sight to attract her attention while having another case hidden in one of the kitchen cabinets that I could drink from without her knowing. I called the case of beer in plain sight my "decoy." When she was in the other room, I would quickly finish the beer I was drinking and then open another, using the dishtowel to muffle the sound of opening a can of beer. I was constantly vigilant about where she was, always calculating how I could drink without her knowing.

Then one night in that small apartment my scheme fell apart. Nicole had gone to bed two hours earlier, and as usual I was free to drink the way I needed to, so I did. I was standing in the kitchen at 11:00 p.m. on a weeknight (we both had to work the next day), chugging a beer when I saw movement out of the corner of my eye. When I turned my head, beer can still at my lips, I saw her peeking around the corner, watching me. A huge pit formed in my stomach, and I once again felt flush as I always did when I was caught. She said, "What the hell are you doing?! It's eleven o'clock on a weeknight and you are chugging beers?!"

There was no excuse which could get me out of this one; I was totally busted. After about ten years of trying to hide my drinking problem from her, there was no doubt it was now exposed and out in the open. An overwhelming sense of shame overtook me, and I finally admitted I had an issue with drinking. She revealed to me that for a long time she suspected I was hiding my drinking from her but never had proof. I committed to "cut back" and I did for a while.

While I was (somewhat) successful at cutting back, here's the catch: moderating my drinking was incredibly frustrating. I tried just drinking on the weekends. The thing is, I was still obsessed with drinking, and during the week I was counting the hours until Friday when I could drink again. When I finally could drink, having one or two beers just didn't get me to where I wanted to be, which was numb. I was irritable all the time.

We moved into our newly built house and soon after had two children. In the new house I saw that I had a plethora of hiding spots for alcohol, so I started with the hiding again. My drinking quickly migrated back to where it was before we lived in the small apartment.

This time around though, Nicole was on to my ways, and it was much harder to hide my drinking from her. So, I moved onto other forms of manipulation. When I got caught drinking, I methodically downplayed the situation. I lied and twisted facts to make her think she was overreacting or that her observations were incorrect.

Sometimes I could tell by the look on her face that she didn't believe me. The thing is, she would still back off from calling me out on my drinking. I realized I didn't have to get her to completely believe my excuses and lies to be successful. All I wanted was for her to stop calling me out. To get her to back down, I just had to sow seeds of doubt in her and make her think she wasn't seeing things correctly.

Even though I became exceptionally good at manipulating her perception, I still got caught every now and then. When that happened, the huge pit in my stomach returned and the familiar feeling of shame would overtake me. I didn't understand why I couldn't just drink like other people.

I deeply loved her and never meant to hurt her, but that drowning feeling made me laser focused on getting what I needed to cope with life: more alcohol. My drive to drink took control of my thinking. The damage I was doing to Nicole, and our relationship simply didn't cross my mind. The disease of addiction had me in the delusion that the only person I was hurting was myself.

In 2014 (the 20th year of our relationship), I awoke one Monday morning with terrible chest pains after yet another weekend of heavy drinking. I thought I was having a heart attack. I still drank that morning as I did every morning before my family woke up. Having drank, I didn't want to draw attention to myself, so I pretended like nothing was happening; got my kids ready for daycare and saw my wife off to work.

Alone in the house with nothing to distract me, my chest pains terrified me. I decided I should go to the hospital. On the way, I called Nicole at her office to let her know what was happening. There was a long pause from her on the other end of the phone. When she finally spoke, she said, "Please, just be honest with yourself and the doctors." My first thought was, "That was a weird thing for her to say when I feel like I am having a heart attack!" Then what she meant hit me. This was all because of the alcohol problem I had been wrestling to hide for over fifteen years. My next thought was, "I guess today is the day."

When I arrived at the hospital, the doctors ran a battery of tests on me, and the results concluded I did not have any heart problems whatsoever. The doctors told me the symptoms I was experiencing were most likely caused by anxiety. That moment was when I finally became honest with myself, the doctors, and nurses about how much I had been drinking. An overwhelming sense of peace came over me; I felt like someone had lifted a heavy boulder off my chest. All the physical pains I was experiencing miraculously disappeared. Perhaps the anxiety was caused by a deep, unconscious notion that I was an alcoholic, and I needed to quit drinking.

That was the day I finally stopped drinking. Today as I reflect, the short phone conversation with Nicole while on the way to the hospital was the moment I hit my final inside rock bottom. I just couldn't live the way I was anymore. There was no big incident, it was the cumulative effects of the small bottoms over the years leading up to that moment. I will expand on what it means to hit "rock bottom" in chapter 3.

I very quickly dove into recovery and really worked hard at it. At first, I thought I had been an alcoholic for maybe five years. The work I did showed me in reality, I had been an alcoholic for fifteen of the twenty years with Nicole.

Nicole also dove into recovery; she went to Al-Anon meetings and did the work they asked her to do. With drinking no longer driving the way I interacted with Nicole; we were finally able to have open and honest communication about what transpired when I was drinking.

She shared with me that my actions while I was drinking hurt her deeply. My delusion that I was only hurting myself while I was drinking was smashed. From our open and honest conversations, I saw a new reality, and it wasn't pretty. I badly hurt the people I loved the most.

I also learned from her that although I kept many facts about my drinking hidden, her gut instinct told her I was lying all those times. She told me that despite not having the hard facts to prove I was abusing alcohol, she knew deep down I was an alcoholic and that I was intentionally manipulating her.

She explained to me that I constantly undermined the very foundation of any loving relationship: trust and honesty. It became clear to me that I had created an emotionally unsafe environment in our relationship. I am regretful about the things I did to her and our relationship while drinking.

Today I am forever grateful that Nicole has sought, and continues to seek, her own recovery from my alcoholism. We are two willing participants who seek recovery together. We both had to work hard at re-establishing trust and emotional connection. We continue to work on repairing the damage done, and we are moving forward into new chapters of our relationship.

* * *

Now Nicole's story.

She shares her experience from her side of our relationship. I ask you to try to find yourself in what she shares regardless of your relationship role with the addict-alcoholic in your life. Try to see where you have had the same or similar experiences as Nicole. Take note of when she reveals how she felt about her situation. Ask yourself: "Have I experienced or felt anything like this?"

* * *

Nicole's story of being in relationship with me as an alcoholic:

"I realized I had become equally as sick as Craig."

Craig and I met at university when I was twenty years old and he was twenty-two. The connection was nearly immediate. We had many interests in common, began dating, and quickly became best friends. We were silly together, emotionally vulnerable with each other, and fell in love. We were into the same music and frequently went to see bands play with our friends. We had our fair share of college drinking, but nothing seemed out of the ordinary at the time.

After graduating college, we entered our corporate careers. We eventually bought a condominium, moved in together and got married. Although we worked long hours Monday through Friday, we took the weekends to still have fun together. We went bike riding, sat on the beach, and still saw our favorite bands play. When we went out on weekend nights together, we of course had a few drinks.

A couple of months after moving in together, every night after work I noticed Craig would have a beer or two … or three. I thought to myself, "OK, so we go out on the weekends and have a few beers and then some beers during Sunday football, but now beers every night after work? That is weird."

Eventually his every-night drinking started to bother me, and I vividly remember asking him one Tuesday evening, "Craig, it's a weeknight and you are drinking multiple beers. Isn't that strange?" His rapid response was sharp, quick, loud, and direct: "Lighten up, Nicole, maybe you should have one too." It was the first time Craig ever acted like that toward me in the five years we had been dating.

His response felt like a blow to my stomach. It shocked me so much that I was speechless. I felt heartbroken and confused. I didn't understand what just happened. I remember thinking,

"What the heck was that and who the hell was that?" What I witnessed was not the Craig I knew. I eventually convinced myself he must have had a difficult day at work and let it go but continued to observe.

Over the next few weeks, I repeatedly witnessed Craig come home from work and down several beers every night. I started to feel angry, confused, and anxious. So, I decided to talk to Craig once again about his everyday drinking. Like before, the sharp, stern, loud voice quickly came out. "Nicole, it's beer, not vodka shots. I'm having a beer or two after work. Chill out." Immediately I had the same stomach-punch feeling I had before, and my heart hurt. I left the room and sobbed. I remember thinking, "Maybe I do need to lighten up; people have a glass of wine after work."

This pattern continued for months, then years. Night after night Craig sat next to me on the couch, drank beers, watched TV, and became emotionally numb. Every time we went out together, I had to drive home because of his drinking. I became disgusted with the beer smell as he lay next to me in bed, and that had never bothered me before. Whenever I mentioned the topic of his drinking, I was repeatedly disregarded with various excuses such as, "Work is a long day," or "People have a glass of wine after work; what's wrong with beer?" He frequently would flip the focus back on me with comments like, "Why don't you look at your control and overachiever issues instead of analyzing my drinking?"

Repeatedly I would hit a breaking point, question Craig, and he would aggressively defend his position with excuses or flip the focus back on me. Then I would leave the room and cry with a broken heart.

As years of this rolled on, two things happened.

First, Craig's silly, sensitive, and intimate side disappeared. Soon the only emotions he showed were anger, judgment of others, and anxiety. I suspected it was because of his drinking.

Second, I developed all sorts of new emotions. I was angry at Craig. I became angry at myself for not being able to let a few beers go. I now felt anxious all the time and couldn't put my finger on why. I decided it was not safe to share my emotions since the nasty Craig could come out which didn't feel good at all. Craig and I were no longer silly together, and intimate conversations disappeared. Our relationship grew distant and transactional.

I developed a lot of inner conflict. My gut told me something wasn't right, and my mind would agree with those instincts. Then Craig's manipulative influences would reshape my thoughts, and then my mind would tell me I was overreacting and maybe I just needed to let go and have some fun. It was like I had two minds, and I didn't know which one to believe. It caused tremendous mental fatigue.

The mixed emotions and mental battles were so exhausting, I developed severe anxiety. I continued to shut down all my emotions and distance myself from Craig. I became controlling over all the little things in life. I now know that was because I felt so out of control in my marriage. So, what was I to do at the time?

Unconsciously, my solution was to busy myself and overachieve in every other area of my life. Although I didn't realize it at the time, I now know that what I was doing was to numb myself from everything happening with Craig. I channeled all my energy into my job and continued to overachieve.

Since I wasn't dealing with my emotions, my inner turmoil got so bad that I went to a therapist. My therapist asked me what I did to take care of myself; she asked what I liked to do for fun. I couldn't identify anything I did for fun. She suggested I find a hobby which would bring me peace and joy.

I did exactly what the therapist said. I found a hobby that brought me peace and joy: horseback riding. Eventually I bought a horse (a large time-commitment hobby) and went riding three or four days a week. While I enjoyed my horse hobby immensely, I started dreading going back home afterwards. So, I spent more and more time at the barn and more time at my job. You see my pattern of avoidance and numbing by staying busy?

Reflecting from where I am today, I also see that my desire to spend more time with my horse and at work wasn't just avoidance and numbing. It was also because that is where I got good feelings. My horse loved me, and my colleagues at work genuinely appreciated me and constantly gave me positive feedback. I wasn't getting any of that at home with Craig. I would go as far as to say I even became "addicted" to my hobby and work for those reasons.

When it came to Craig's drinking, I never counted how many drinks he had or paid attention to the amount of alcohol that came in and out of the house. I knew he was drinking every day, but I didn't realize how much. This all changed when we decided to build a house, and we sold our condo. While the house was under construction, we moved into a small apartment.

In the small apartment there was no place for Craig to hide his alcohol, so the situation was right in front of me and became much clearer. I would observe a new case of beer coming in and disappearing in twenty-four hours. Once again, my gut told me something was very wrong, but my mind told me it was only beer, and you can't be an alcoholic with just beer, right?

At one point, I confronted Craig with the hard facts I now had about his drinking. Although he got visibly agitated, he said he would cut back, that it wasn't a big deal. I had a nagging feeling in my gut that it was a big problem, and that he wasn't going to be able to cut back without help. Then my mind would again talk me out of what my instincts were telling me. I came to the realization there was nothing I could do to force him to change.

We eventually had two children, and the focus became the kids. Having children created a new bond between us which felt good since not much bonding had occurred in years. The thing is, Craig continued to get more anxious and irritable in life. He had other behavioral changes too. He would take longer than needed to do simple tasks like bringing the trash out or getting firewood. My gut feeling told me that although he appeared to have cut back, he was in reality just hiding his drinking from me. Some days I would ask, "What took so long?" As usual an angry response would come back my way. Other days I was too exhausted and mentally beaten down by his excuses to even inquire.

I eventually got to a breaking point where I couldn't handle it anymore; something had to change. I had thoughts of taking the kids and leaving Craig. With all the things I had going on between work, the kids, and doing everything around the house, the decision of divorcing Craig was overwhelming and too hard to figure out, so I ignored it.

The end of his drinking finally came one day. While I was at work I got a call from Craig. He was driving to the hospital be-

cause he was having bad chest pains. He thought he was having a heart attack. My gut instinct told me it was not a heart attack; it was anxiety over drinking. A calmness I hadn't felt in a long time came over me, and I finally listened to my intuition. I said to him, "I love you, Craig; please just be honest with yourself and the doctors. I will stop by on my way home from work." That is where I left it; I said nothing about his drinking. When I hung up the phone, I felt a small bit of peace I hadn't felt in years. He was in good hands at the hospital, and I didn't have to worry.

After work I stopped by the hospital. When I walked into his room, Craig said to me for the first time, "I have a drinking problem, and the doctors are helping me." I sat with him for a bit, gave him a hug and kiss, and told him, "You can do this; ask for help." Then I left to take care of the kids.

My behavior on that day was completely calm and clear, out of character from who I had become from over fifteen years of living with Craig as an active alcoholic. I now know the peace I felt was because the previously hidden truths about how bad Craig's drinking was, which my instincts were telling me all along and I ignored, were finally out in the open.

The next day Craig was released from the hospital, and he came back to the house. At that point, my controlling, fix-it personality kicked into overdrive. I felt he could not live at home and he needed to go to a rehabilitation center. Despite having a two- and a four-year-old at home and working full time, I started researching rehab centers for him. Craig decided he didn't need rehab; he would try attending Alcoholics Anonymous (AA) meetings.

I didn't feel comfortable with his plan. I really thought he needed some more professional help. My "Super Woman" response kicked in again, and I wanted to make sure he would stay sober (as if I had control). I thought, "Wow, thank God he stopped drinking; everything is going to be easy now." I just need to make sure he stays this way. For some reason I felt a huge obligation to support his sobriety. I soon took on many of his household chores to make sure he had time to go to AA meetings every night after work. He also played basketball, and I thought exercise would be good for him, so I made sure he was able to go to that.

Then something completely unexpected for me happened. When he was drinking, I was anxious and controlling because his drinking was out of control. However, he was home every night, at least able to help around the house and with our two children. Then when he got sober, he was out at AA meetings every night. Now I was anxious, controlling, angry, and add to that list overwhelmed because I felt like, "Why is this more work for me?!" I actually felt more anxious and physically exhausted now that he was sober! I expected things to get better, and it wasn't making sense!

Looking back, I realized I was doing absolutely nothing to take care of myself. Three months into Craig's sobriety he convinced me to try Al-Anon. At the very first Al-Anon meeting I went to, they read aloud Steps 1-3 of Al-Anon's 12 Steps.

In particular, step 1 hit me like a ton of bricks:

Step 1: "We admitted we were powerless over alcohol—that our lives had become unmanageable."

When that was read, I wept. They were tears of relief; it was like a black cloud had been lifted off me. I realized my life was completely unmanageable; I was trying to control everything I possibly could. It was exhausting. I came to understand I was in fact powerless over alcohol (Craig's drinking).

After Step 1 was read, somebody in the meeting then rephrased Step 1 saying, "I am powerless over people, places and things." It was then I understood I was powerless over Craig's life, and I couldn't control him even outside of the drinking. The biggest revelation was I only had control over myself and how I reacted to what life presented me.

I continued to attend one or two Al-Anon meetings per week for the next couple of years, all the while working full time, supporting Craig with his daily AA meetings, and taking care of two kids. The people in the Al-Anon meetings were incredibly welcoming, and they would share very personal stories. I felt less alone; I was surrounded by a group of people who understood what I was going through. They helped me see the impact of living with an active alcoholic for over fifteen years.

Some of the key things I learned and realized were:

- *I had no knowledge I was living with an active alcoholic or that alcoholism was so much more than just drinking too much.*
- *I had no knowledge or support on how to create healthy boundaries with Craig.*
- *I didn't realize I was not taking care of myself.*
- *I had many more emotions deep down that I wasn't in touch with. In addition to the anger, I realized I also felt tremendous mother guilt for not protecting my children from Craig's alcoholism.*

- *As a result of all this, I realized I had become equally as sick as Craig.*

The people in Al-Anon helped me see that Craig's lying, manipulation, and distancing in our relationship caused me to emotionally shut down and stuff my feelings. My solution of staying busy so I wouldn't have to think or feel made my life unmanageable. It caused me to become very controlling of all the little things in my life since I didn't feel emotionally safe in my marriage. Worst of all, I completely lost my internal compass, that gut feeling which used to guide me through life.

I have come to realize recovery is not just for Craig. Recovery is a process for both of us. It's been ten years of peeling back the layers in my healing process. Gradually I have started to feel safe and allow myself to feel my feelings. I must get in touch with how I feel now as well as dig down to all those stuffed emotions from my fifteen years of living with an active alcoholic.

We both work hard at our recovery. It is a journey with twists and turns ... with ugly moments and moments of peace. I have learned to feel again. I have learned to trust my gut instinct again. I have learned to express my feelings, albeit not always in a productive way, and I am working on that! I am learning how to effectively communicate and create healthy boundaries.

We are rebuilding our marriage together. Craig and I continue to work on healing ourselves, and we are developing a new honest, emotionally safe, and intimate marriage. As I heal the emotions, my memories are being transformed from emotionally charged, sad memories to nuggets of wisdom which I am learning to be grateful for.

* * *

My story shows how, when in the grip of addiction, good people can do bad things to those they love the most. Along with that comes the delusion addict-alcoholics frequently believe, that the only person they are hurting is themselves. In the throes of addiction, I never considered the deep emotional effects my behavior was having on Nicole.

The lack of detail on all the things I did to Nicole in my story demonstrates that my manipulation had become so automatic and pervasive that I don't remember it. I also don't have a clear memory because I was drunk or high most of the time. It took honest and open conversations with Nicole to come to realize all the things I did to her.

When you are in a relationship with an addict-alcoholic, each of you experiences a different reality.

Nicole's story was quite different than mine. The first big difference is the amount of detail she shared. Her story shows that as a loved one you remember much more detail from the experience than the addict-alcoholic does because:

1. The loved ones like you are not drunk or high when the situations occur, so your memory is not impaired.
2. The addict-alcoholic's manipulation creates emotional trauma, which burns those experiences into your memory.

Nicole also described very well the subtleties of addict-alcoholic manipulation. Things such as voice tone, voice volume, flipping the focus back on you, and lame excuses all have a profound effect on you. She shared intimate details on how my behavior affected her mentally and emotionally. She made it clear that when you have an active addict-alcoholic in your life, your relationship with them becomes a tangled mess of emotions and self-doubt. Life with an addict-alcoholic will cause you all kinds of negative emotions like stress, anxiety, irritability, or depression. Those negative emotions even lead to physical symptoms as you will see in some of the stories in later chapters. Nicole described how recovery is also for people like you so you may heal from the emotional trauma.

Can you relate to any of the experiences or feelings Nicole shared with you? In the next section, I have many more questions for you to further connect with your personal situation!

HAVE YOU EVER?

Have you ever …

- Worried that a beloved person in your life drinks too much or is taking drugs?
- Thought if you were a better partner to your loved one, they wouldn't drink or use drugs?
- Felt overwhelmed because your addicted partner is incapable, and you feel like you are single-handedly responsible for running the household?
- Lost sleep worrying about your child's drinking or drugging?
- Wondered where you went wrong as a parent, causing your child to become an addict-alcoholic?

- Been annoyed or angry with an addicted sibling over how much they take advantage of your parents?
- Felt bad for your parents because of what your addicted sibling is putting them through?
- Worried whether or not your addicted sibling will show up drunk or high to family events?
- Felt like you were alone or abandoned as a child because your addicted parent wasn't present for you?
- Been disgusted with an addicted parent because you had to be the adult in the relationship?
- Had a gut feeling your loved one was lying but you couldn't prove it?
- Lied to somebody else about how much your loved one drinks or that they take drugs?
- Counted empty beer bottles or measured and marked liquor bottles?
- Searched through your loved one's car, bureau, toolbox, purse, or backpack looking for a stash of drugs or alcohol?
- Looked at your loved one's phone to see with whom they had been texting?
- Made excuses for your loved one to other people?
- Followed your loved one somewhere because you thought they were lying about where they were going?
- Tried to control everything in your life?

- Thought for sure you heard your loved one slur, and you didn't say anything to them about it?
- Seen your loved one become overly defensive or angry when you asked a simple question about their drinking or using?
- Thought your loved one's eyes looked glassy or bloodshot, but they denied having taken anything?
- Had your loved one convince you to give them money for something important like rent, only to find out they spent it on drugs or alcohol?
- Ever asked the local liquor store owner if your loved one has been there?
- Blamed someone or something else for your addicted loved one's using?
- Incessantly talked about the addict-alcoholic with other family members or friends every time you got together or had a phone call?
- Heard your phone ring and feared it was the police or the hospital calling about your addicted loved one?

If you can identify with Nicole's story or any of the questions mentioned above, then *Beyond the Lies* is for you. You may not realize it, but your life is being shaped by the addict-alcoholic. Living with an addict-alcoholic causes you to constantly doubt and question yourself.

Please know that you are not alone.

I want to recover with you, and I promise we will walk through this together. I am going to help you understand why you feel the way you do so you may finally move forward and have the life you want.

CHAPTER 2:

Beyond the Lies

2.1 WHY I WROTE BEYOND THE LIES

I was an active addict-alcoholic for more than fifteen years. I got sober in 2014. Early in my recovery journey, my oldest brother, Glenn, was still an active addict-alcoholic. He was a very heavy user, and he was constantly in the hospital with pancreatitis. All the health problems caused by his drinking and using drugs did not stop him. I really thought I was going to see him die from the disease of addiction. So did his partner Eileen, with whom he lived. Eileen shares her complete story later in this book.

I would get frequent calls from Eileen about my brother. She called to ask me questions about Glenn, to try to make sense of his behavior. She would say things to me like,

- "Your brother claimed he wasn't using, but he just didn't seem right."
- "I just feel it in my gut that he isn't being honest with me."

- "I don't believe him, but I have no proof he is lying."

She had no idea how much he was controlling her because addict-alcoholics are experts at manipulation. I would ask her to describe what happened. As she spoke, I found myself knowing right away what my brother was up to behind the scenes *because when I was actively using, I did those same things to my partner.* I would confirm what her gut instinct was telling her by explaining what he was really up to. Basically, I became her "secret decoder ring" for my brother's behavior. We had many phone calls over a period of a year or two, having different conversations about different incidents as they happened.

Fortunately, my brother eventually got sober and sought recovery with the same vigor with which he chased drugs and alcohol. I am delighted to have my brother back! The two of them are still together, and Eileen is tremendously grateful for all the phone conversations we had. She said after talking to me on the phone she realized she could not do this alone; she needed support. She told me that my support was critical to her well-being by helping her navigate the difficult and confusing landscape of living with an active alcoholic.

Recovery resources for the addict-alcoholic are vast, and health insurance even pays for much of the support. Over time I realized in working with the family and friends of addict-alcoholics, similar resources are not readily available to people like you, the loved ones of addict-alcoholics.

This huge gap in resources for the loved ones of addict-alcoholics stood out to me. As I reflected upon the experience with Glenn and Eileen, I felt a calling to extend what I did for her to all the loved ones of addict-alcoholics out there who feel isolated, alone, and confused: people like you. This is why *Beyond the Lies* has come into existence. The intention of this book is to fill that gap for you.

Regardless of whether the addict-alcoholic is a partner, parent, child, sibling, or friend, the fact is that having lived with an addict-alcoholic, you have been deeply affected by the disease of addiction as well. The secondhand effects of addiction and alcoholism are as real as the effects of secondhand smoke. This may be hard for you to accept; after all, it's obvious the addict-alcoholic is the one who needs the help, right? The knowledge you gain from *Beyond the Lies* will facilitate an understanding of the many ways you have been affected by the addict-alcoholic in your life. Essentially, you will be shown root causes for why you feel the way you do.

I have found from talking to many loved ones like you that a lot of the things I will tell you about addiction and addict-alcoholics are not known to you. For your own sanity, it is important to understand how these characteristics affect you.

The purpose of *Beyond the Lies* is:

- To discuss some of the lesser-known characteristics of the addict-alcoholic, and about addiction in general. This will give you a baseline working knowledge of addiction and how the addict-alcoholic operates.
- To help you by giving you the "secret decoder ring" to the behavior of the addict-alcoholic in your life.
- To show you how their behavior affects you.
- To help you create change in your relationship with the addict-alcoholic.

2.2 WHERE DID THE INFORMATION IN THIS BOOK COME FROM?

As I shared earlier, I grew up in a household with family members who were active alcoholics and addicts. Despite knowing firsthand what addiction does to the family, I still became one myself. Graced to find recovery, I have taken a long journey to get to where I am today. In this journey, I have been to thousands of recovery meetings and worked with many family members and friends of addict-alcoholics.

I have found that most loved ones and friends of addict-alcoholics go to great lengths to try and help, often sacrificing their own well-being. Their efforts are with good intention, yet many of the things the loved ones do to help don't help at all. Unbeknownst to the loved ones, people like you, their actions may even be enabling the addict-alcoholic to drink and use drugs. There is a fine line between helping and enabling. A detailed discussion on enabling will come in section 4.6.

This book is born from my own experience and other people's experiences. The things you will read about really happened to real people like you. We all know that experience is the best teacher. I will share with you many real personal stories. They are my own experiences as well as those of others who have given me permission to share their stories with you. Other than stories from my immediate family members, the names have been changed to respect their identity.

Beyond the Lies is based on:

- What I personally did to my loved ones while I was an active addict-alcoholic.
- My partner Nicole's experiences and perspective from living with me during my active years and in recovery.

- Thousands of stories I have heard from other addict-alcoholics as an involved member of the recovery community.
- Interviews and interactions with addict-alcoholics, their partners, their family, and their friends.

While you read this book, please keep the following things in mind:

- *Active* is used to describe an addict-alcoholic who is currently using or drinking.
- The words *using, drinking,* and *drugging* are used interchangeably. Although in the recovery community, using and drugging typically refers to drugs, and drinking of course to alcohol, please extend whatever term is used to fit your situation whether it's drugs or alcohol.
- *Booze, alcohol, drugs, chemicals, substances* are also used interchangeably. Some of the stories shared with you are specific to alcohol or a certain drug. Please don't let the specific substance mentioned make you think the content is not relevant to your situation. There is a saying in the recovery community: "Identify, don't compare." This means, take the essence of what is being described and apply it to your experience.

I don't claim to be an expert. I do want to share my experience with you. Some people may not agree with everything I have to say and that is perfectly OK! My hope in sharing this with you is to

- broaden your perspective concerning the addict-alcoholic in your life,

- answer some of the questions you may have, and even answer questions you didn't know you had,
- open up dialogues which may not have happened otherwise, and
- show you some potential paths forward.

2.3 A WARNING TO YOU

I want to let you know that you may experience many emotions while reading *Beyond the Lies.* As you journey through this book, you will learn about many things which you may not have realized were happening in your life. For example, how much the addict-alcoholic in your life has controlled you and how they did it. Your feelings about the situation—whatever they may be—are valid and you are not alone.

Some of what you learn might bring up feelings of anger, sadness, or rage. As you read you may feel heartbroken or disgusted. You are not alone if this happens! While I was writing this book, some of the people who helped me edit it felt those very things as they reflected on how the topics happened in their own lives.

It is normal to experience these emotions. Allow yourself to feel them. Letting the emotions flow is the doorway for you to be free from all the trauma of living with an addict-alcoholic.

Finally, know that even though the addict-alcoholic may have done bad things to you, they are not a bad person. They are a sick person with a disease called addiction.

CHAPTER 3:

Addiction Is More than Drinking or Using Too Much

3.1 INTRODUCTION

In my experience, it has been amazing to see how the disease of addiction is still not well understood by the general population. This is true despite many decades of study by the science and psychology community. Even more amazing is how much the people living with addict-alcoholics (people like you) don't understand the disease of addiction. If family members and friends had a better understanding of the addict-alcoholic, years and even decades of pain could potentially be spared.

This overview is by no means the complete story; there are volumes of books written on the science and psychology of addiction. You will gain a baseline understanding of addiction and some perspective on the thought processes of addict-alcoholics. Hopefully, what I share will help you better understand them, and how their disease of addiction affects you.

3.2 ARE YOU IN TOUCH WITH HOW YOU THINK AND FEEL ABOUT THIS?

I invite you to actively answer the questions below. They will help you get in touch with your thoughts and feelings about the situation with your loved one who is an addict-alcoholic. For me, writing down things like this helps me solidify them in my mind and clarify my experiences. Reflecting on the questions in writing or with family/friends is the beginning of your healing. The addict-alcoholic will knock you off balance mentally and emotionally to prevent you from speaking up to them about their drinking and using. They do this by instilling doubt and uncertainty, convincing you to believe them and not your own observations and intuition. They cause you to question:

- what you saw (red or glassy eyes or a stumble),
- what you smelled on them (alcohol or drugs),
- what you heard from them (slurred speech or what sounds like a lie),
- what you already know about them (they are using much of the time), and
- most importantly, your own intuition (intuitive thoughts or "gut feelings" tell you the truth without "proof").

Writing your responses to the questions will help you remember and validate what you already know! Take a little time to ponder and answer the following questions to the best of your ability:

1. How would you personally define what an addict or alcoholic is?
2. Why do you think the addict-alcoholics use drugs or alcohol the way they do?
3. How does the addict-alcoholic in your life control and manipulate you? Name some specific ways.
4. Are you in touch with how you feel about your situation?
    - Write down a few emotions you feel when you are around the addict-alcoholic in your life.
    - Write down what problem(s) you are experiencing in response to these emotions.
    - In two-three sentences, write what it would feel like to solve the problem(s).
    - Write down the one question you would like to get answered by the addict-alcoholic in your life.

3.3 ADDICTION IS A DISEASE, NOT A MORAL ISSUE OR CHARACTER FLAW

Addiction was declared an illness in 1956 by the American Medical Association (AMA). In 1987 the AMA upgraded it to a disease, confirming that addiction is not a moral issue. The latest term, Alcohol Use Disorder (AUD) was introduced in the Diagnostic and Statistical Manual of Mental Disorders in 2013. Just so there is no confusion, AUD is the same thing as alcoholism, they are just different terms for the same illness.

The key is, regardless of what term you prefer or use, addiction is recognized by the medical and scientific community as an illness.

Despite these declarations, addiction and alcoholism still carry a stigma of shame and embarrassment for both the addict-alcoholic and their loved ones.

Many addict-alcoholics exhibit an apparent lack of self-control or even do immoral things such as lie, cheat, steal, or commit violence. A deficiency of morals or self-discipline is not the cause of these behaviors; the disease of addiction is the cause. When a person is addicted, there is an overwhelming drive to drink and drug at all costs. Using drugs and alcohol becomes the single most important thing in their life, above family and above work.

I am not saying the addict-alcoholic should not be held accountable for their behavior because they have a disease. Rather, I am saying that the root cause of their behavior is that they have a disease. I have heard many addict-alcoholics say: "That wasn't me, that was my disease." Although this may be true, it does not mean they shouldn't feel the consequences of their behavior.

WHAT DOES THIS HAVE TO DO WITH YOU?

If you did not know addiction is officially a disease, you are like most people! I wanted to make sure you knew addiction is officially a disease because without that knowledge you may be left with the long-propagated misconception that addiction means your loved one is weak in character or a moral failure. For many like you, that misconception comes with shame and embarrassment.

Let me ask you this:

- Would you be angry at them for having type 1 diabetes or some other disease?
- Would you feel shame or embarrassment if they have this other disease?
- Would you hold back seeking help and guidance from friends or professionals when it comes to other diseases?

Addiction is a complex mental, emotional and physical disease (or disorder), not a moral failing or a lack of self-control.

Most people like you would answer no to these questions. So, why is the disease of addiction different than any other disease (like type 1 diabetes)?

In *Beyond the Lies* we are going to dive deep into what it looks and feels like to live with someone who has the disease of addiction. Experts have called the disease of addiction a "family disease." You will see that you are not alone in what you are feeling and experiencing. There is help and hope out there for both the addict-alcoholic and you!

3.4 THE SHAME WITH THE WORDS ADDICT AND ALCOHOLIC (IT'S A FAMILY AFFAIR)

Let's start with an experience I had with my mother.

* * *

My story about my mom's shame:

"Even as a career registered nurse she fell victim to addiction shame."

When I was in high school in the '80s, my dad got sober. My dad dove headfirst into recovery, and I remember my parents discussing what he had learned in rehab and through recovery meetings. My mom was a career Registered Nurse. She seemed to fully accept that alcoholism was considered a disease (the term used at the time) and that my dad was not a bad person for being an alcoholic. So, they both had this intellectual knowledge.

Fast forward about ten years and my dad was still going strong in recovery. I frequently heard my parents have discussions around addiction and recovery, they talked to each other openly about it inside our house. Outside of the house was another story; I never heard them discuss any of these topics openly.

My cousin was getting married, and our family was invited...all seven of us! We all went except my oldest brother; he was a no-show. My mom told the four of us siblings who were present, and all our relatives, that he was absent because he was in the hospital with diabetes.

I came to find out almost twenty years later that my oldest brother wasn't at the wedding because he was in rehab. In fact, he never even had diabetes. Despite my dad being next to her for all those years as a great example of recovery, she lied to all of us. Here was my mom, a medical professional, who had the knowledge that the American Medical Association officially declared addiction a disease. Yet, she just couldn't seem to tell anyone that my oldest brother was an alcoholic who needed help and was getting it. Even as a career registered nurse she fell victim to addiction shame.

* * *

Today, with thirty more years of scientific progress on addiction since my mom did that, I continue to see similar behaviors in recovery meetings. Sometimes, I see newcomers who have lost so much because of substance abuse: they've been fired, their partner left them, their kids won't talk to them, all their friends want nothing to do with them. Despite their situation, sometimes they still can't seem to use the words *addict* or *alcoholic* in reference to themselves. It's as if saying those words will somehow bring them to a new low.

Why is this?

Shame.

Shame comes with addiction, especially with using the dreaded words addict or alcoholic. Even with the well-known scientific knowledge today that addiction is a disease (or a disorder, whichever term you prefer), the reality is, many people, including the family and friends of addicts and alcoholics, experience addiction shame. The shame comes from the bad things they may have done in the grip of addiction. The shame also comes from a deep feeling that despite what science says, they still feel like an addict or alcoholic is a weak or immoral person for falling victim to addiction.

Someone can tell me not to feel shame because addiction is a "disease" or a "disorder." My head may say, "Yes, I agree." Yet, why do I still feel shame? We will get to the answer further down.

The key thing here is that despite the intellectual knowledge which exists today, you or your loved one with a substance abuse problem may still feel shameful. If you relate to this, know it is totally normal.

As I interviewed family members and friends of addicts and alcoholics for this project, I noticed many of them had difficulty referring to their addicted loved one with the words *addict* or *alcoholic.* Keep in mind these people agreed to talk to me because they have been impacted by an addict or alcoholic in their life. Still, some of them were unable to use these words.

The tragedy of shame is that it traps you in a self-imposed prison.

One man in his forties I interviewed who has an alcoholic mother discussed how she tries to manipulate him *all the time,* continues to impact the family with incidents because of her drinking, and how he had to cut her off from seeing his daughter. He still would not use alcoholic to describe her. The furthest he would go was to say: "She drinks a little too much wine all the time." I share his complete story in later sections.

Knowing intellectually that addiction is a disease or disorder doesn't mean you won't feel shame and embarrassment. A lot of societal shame and embarrassment still exist around addiction, making it difficult for many people to use the terms *addict* or *alcoholic.*

The tragedy of shame is that it traps us in a self-imposed prison. Shame prevents you from helping yourself because the shame keeps you from talking openly and seeking help, allowing the disease (or disorder) of addiction to propagate around you. This applies to the loved ones as much as it does the addict or alcoholic.

Shame prevents you from helping others who may be going through the same thing because you don't share your life experience with them.

What I want you to know is this:

You have the power to dissolve the shame and embarrassment.

It may take time and work, but you can heal and be free of shame and embarrassment. So, back to the question above of "Why do I still feel shame?"

The answer is:

Lack of acceptance.

I am not talking about accepting the intellectual knowledge that addiction is a disease or disorder. I can read scientific books and listen to scientific talks on addiction all I want. What I have learned in recovery is that true acceptance is in the heart, not the head. So, try to accept in your heart that addiction does not make someone a bad person, they are not a moral failure or a person of weak character.

Lack of acceptance creates insecurities over who and what we are. Shame is a protection mechanism that keeps us quiet to protect our insecurities from being exposed. Moving toward acceptance is what dissolves shame, because in acceptance, there are no more insecurities to protect.

When the shame dissolves, we are free. Free to share and help others. Free to help others come to acceptance in their own hearts and help them break out of their own prison of shame.

I can tell you in my recovery, shame has been healed within me. I was blessed for this to happen very early in my journey. Without the handcuffs of shame, I became free to be open about what I have been through as an addict and alcoholic. This freedom has allowed me to help many people who would never have known I was somebody they could talk to.

Check out this story of an interaction I had with a work colleague.

* * *

My story about overcoming shame:

"You gave me the strength to try sobriety."

It was January 2015, and I was about three months sober. I was at an annual sales meeting for my company in Toronto, Canada. These sales meetings used to be total blowout drinking frenzies for me (hey, the booze was free!). It was the end of the day, and time for cocktail hour. Being so early on in recovery, I decided it would be wise to go to a recovery meeting instead of the cocktail hour.

In the elevator on my way out, a colleague I had a personal relationship with got on a few floors down. I had my winter coat on, yet the cocktail hour was in the hotel. So, seeing my coat, he asked: "Where are you going?" I answered: "I'm just going out." He pressed on: "Well, where? What are you doing?" I caved in and said: "I just got sober and I'm going to an AA meeting."

After that, an uncomfortable silence followed the rest of the way down. As the elevator doors opened, he wished me well, but it was awkward.

One year later, I was in Spain at yet another annual sales meeting and still sober. At dinner one night, a colleague came up to me and said: "Hey, someone told me you know something about this." He very discreetly (and embarrassingly) showed me an AA meeting schedule booklet. I replied: "I do know something about that. Who told you this?" He looked at me funny and said: "You did! Remember? Last year in the elevator in Toronto?" I had totally forgotten about that quick exchange in the elevator.

He went on to say: "You didn't know, but I was really struggling with drinking; it was causing problems for me at home. When you shared you were an alcoholic and you were sober, it was a huge punch in the gut for me. Your timing couldn't have been better. You gave me the strength to try sobriety." We proceeded to talk about recovery for the next hour, and he even asked me to sponsor him in AA. He was able to accept that he was an alcoholic and has since become sober.

At the time, I still had some remaining addiction shame even though I was in recovery. It made me paranoid that I would be judged by my colleagues. So, I "tightened up" things at work and moving forward I didn't tell anybody.

* * *

Now, nine years later, I have made more progress getting over my own shame and embarrassment. The healing has enabled me to write this book and share these stories to help as many people as possible.

WHAT DOES THIS HAVE TO DO WITH YOU?

One of the reasons I am discussing this topic is because the words alcoholic and addict appear a lot in *Beyond the Lies.* If those words bother you, try to remember when I use the words, they are simply a statement of fact, with no negative emotions attached to them. The words come with no moral labels or judgment.

The tragedy of shame and embarrassment is that those emotions are a self-imposed prison. Putting yourself in this prison results in the following:

- Allows the disease of addiction to propagate around you because the feelings can prevent you from talking about it and seeking help.
- Prevents you from helping other loved ones of addict-alcoholics going through the same things you have.

Remember, you have the power to dissolve shame and embarrassment through acceptance in your heart that addiction is not a moral failure. Take Nicole and me, for instance. We have not only recovered from active addiction in the household, we have also healed the shame and embarrassment in us. Without those emotional handcuffs, we are now free to be open about what we went through. The emotional freedom has allowed us to help many people who would never have known we were people they could talk to. Getting over our own shame and embarrassment has enabled us to bring you Beyond the Lies to help as many people as possible!

For you addicts, alcoholics, and loved ones of users out there, please do yourself and those you may be able to help a favor:

Break out of whatever prison of shame you are holding yourself in!

Accept in your heart that you are not a lesser person, bad person or immoral for whatever you are ashamed about (this goes beyond addiction). It is so very freeing, clearing the way for you to be of maximum service to those who may benefit from your experiences.

What if shame kept me from sharing my experience with that guy in the elevator? Where would he be now? You never know when it might be just the right time to make a difference in someone else's life.

3.5 ADDICT-ALCOHOLICS ARE NOT JUST IN *DENIAL*, THEY ARE ALSO IN A *DELUSION*

One of the most common phrases you may have heard or used about addict-alcoholics is: "They are totally in denial!" Most of the time, this is an incomplete assessment. Usually, mixed in with denial is its more pervasive sibling: delusion. For you people reading this who may be the loved one of an addict-alcoholic, can you identify with anything similar to the following questions?

- Has the addict-alcoholic in your life ever been convinced that a person or an outside circumstance was the cause of their problematic situation, but to you it was clearly caused by their drinking or using?

- Have you ever confronted the addict-alcoholic about their drinking or using and their confident response was: "I am not that bad" or "I can stop anytime I want"?
- Have you ever witnessed outlandish behavior at a party or restaurant, and the addict-alcoholic didn't think it to be so?
- Have you ever had an argument over who will drive home because, despite being high or drunk, they had the conviction they were OK to drive? If you ended up driving, did the addict-alcoholic sulk, become irritated, or yell at you?
- Have you ever caught your addict-alcoholic drunk or high and they blamed someone or something else for why they used?
- Can you think of any other incidents in your experience where the addict-alcoholic was clearly in the wrong but seemed to truly believe what they were saying?
- Have you ever felt like your addict or alcoholic is living in a different reality?

If you answered "yes" to any of the questions above, then you have witnessed addict-alcoholic delusion.

Delusion is much trickier than denial because it clouds perception. I want to clearly explain the difference so let's define the two. According to the Merriam-Webster dictionary:

Denial:

1. Refusal to admit the truth or reality of something.[1]

1 "denial." *Merriam-Webster.com*, 2025. https://www.merriam-webster.com.

Delusion:

1. Something that is falsely or delusively believed or propagated,
2. A persistent false psychotic belief regarding the self.......... that is maintained despite INDESPUTABLE evidence to the contrary.[2]

Let's exemplify the difference through an analogy. The addict-alcoholic wakes up in the morning; they look out their window and it's raining. They don't like the fact that it's raining.

- In a denial, the addict-alcoholic will refuse to acknowledge it's raining by simply pulling down the window shade.
- In a delusion, the addict-alcoholic puts on a special pair of glasses which, only for them, filters the image coming through and makes it look like a nice sunny day.

In short, a denial is a lie, the truth is known and rejected. A delusion is something the person believes to be true, even when the evidence everyone else sees clearly says it is false. Delusion amounts to a distorted perception of reality.

From the thousands of stories (literally thousands!) I have heard in recovery meetings, some of the most common delusions addict-alcoholics believe are:

- *"I am not that bad."* Frequently addict-alcoholics hang around with people who use drugs and alcohol more than they do, and this supports the delusional thought

2 "delusion." *Merriam-Webster.com,* 2025. https://www.merriam-webster.com.

that their own using isn't that bad. Has the addict-alcoholic in your life ever pointed out someone else and said: "At least I am not as bad as them"? I totally did this. If my wife confronted me, I would even rat out my friends by pointing out how drunk they were.

- *"I have control over my using."* I thought I had control because I wasn't one of those alcoholics who always drank until they passed out or blacked out. I could stop drinking when I got to the state I wanted to be in…numb! To me it "proved" I wasn't alcoholic. Mind you, the state of numbness came after twelve to fifteen beers and a few joints…every day. Doesn't seem like control now as I look at it from a sober place!
- *"I am not an addict-alcoholic."* One speaker I heard at a recovery meeting talked about doing service work at hospitals for alcoholic patients with failing livers, literally swollen like a football sticking out of their side. Many of these people still vigorously defended that their condition was not because of the alcohol.
- *"My drinking/using is not hurting anyone else but me."* I was a highly functioning drunk by outside-looking-in standards. I actually excelled at my job and was a happy drunk…so where was the harm? After I got sober my wife lovingly pointed out to me that when drinking, I was completely unavailable emotionally, and she felt very alone. Now in my recovery (our recovery!) we have been learning how to reconnect.
- *"I am getting away with my using; nobody around me knows how much I am drinking and using."* I totally had

this delusion when I was drinking and using. I thought I was the smartest guy in the world with my expert hiding and sneaking skills. I thought nobody knew. Although I very rarely got caught in the act of drinking and using, I found out once I got sober and had real conversations with my wife that she always knew. The giveaway? When I drank, my personality changed. I became mellow and disconnected.

- *"My using is not causing my problems."* See my "if only" statements a few paragraphs below for some examples!
- *"I can quit anytime I want."* It is rare when an addict-alcoholic can stop anytime they want. Physical addiction means that if they stop, they will have withdrawal symptoms, which can be harrowing and dangerous. Even when they aren't harrowing, they are very uncomfortable, and this is a huge barrier to "stopping anytime I want." Here is a short story from me on this.

* * *

My story about the first time I tried to stop drinking:

"I never considered that maybe I had become physically addicted."

It was the year 2000, Nicole and I had just bought a condo and moved in together for the first time. I knew I was drinking too much, and Nicole would not be happy if she found out. My thought was that I just needed to "grow up" and stop drinking so much. I never considered that I had become physically addicted.

So, the first day we moved in together I stopped drinking. We were young, didn't have much money and we didn't hire movers. I did it all myself. Despite being utterly exhausted from all the physical work, I could not fall asleep that night. Every time I looked at the clock on the nightstand, it was another hour later and I hadn't slept a wink. I had to work the next day, and at 2:00 a.m. my solution was to go downstairs and chug four beers. It worked.

The next day as I reflected on what happened I realized I was physically addicted to alcohol. The realization was absolutely horrifying because it meant that maybe, just maybe, I had a drinking problem. I couldn't just quit anytime I wanted, and it scared the hell out of me…but it would be another 14 years of wrestling with trying to control my drinking until I finally got sober.

* * *

For an active addict-alcoholic, the self-delusion will persist even when they are not high or drunk. Their delusion causes their perception to be constantly skewed.

Having now explained delusion to you, it is my observation that most addict-alcoholics live in a combination of delusion and denial. Know that even a small amount of self-delusion creates thought patterns which make it difficult for them to recognize the truth of their situation.

When addict-alcoholics experience the consequences of their behavior, self-delusion will prevent them from recognizing addiction as the root cause of their problems. They will constantly blame outside forces for their problems—anything but the chemicals. I call this the "if only's":

- If only I had more money, I wouldn't have this worry. (Blaming their using on worry.)
- If only my boss wasn't such a jerk, I wouldn't have been fired. (When really, they were fired for poor performance because of using.)
- If only my partner cared about me, I would be happier. (Blaming their using on unhappiness.)
- If only the police officer hadn't singled me out, I wouldn't have lost my driver's license. (They flat out got caught driving under the influence.)

Most addict-alcoholics live in a combination of delusion and denial.

Applied broadly, self-delusion means they will find false reasons to lessen the severity of their substance abuse as a whole. I discussed this in the first bullet of common delusions above ("I am not that bad"). If the addict-alcoholic has ever pointed to someone worse than they are and said, "I am not as bad as them," then you have witnessed them trying to support their delusion that they are "not that bad."

In a narrow view, self-delusion skews their perception of specific situations or incidents so their drinking or using is not to blame. Any time something bad happens (even things like getting fired, divorced, or arrested), they will blame it on someone or something as the cause, and they believe it.

SO, WHY ARE ADDICT-ALCOHOLICS IN A DELUSION?

Why are addict-alcoholics in a self-created delusion? The answer is fear. For all human beings, fear triggers our fight-or-flight response, which is a survival response. For the addict-alcoholic, it's emotional survival which is at stake. Their fear is born from the thought of giving up their main tool for coping: chemicals. The fear is so great they create a delusion as a protection mechanism. In the delusion, they convince themselves that their problems are caused by anything but using drugs and alcohol (their main tool for coping). Essentially, when in this delusion they are blinded from being able to see the root cause of their current problems is addiction.

WHAT DOES THIS HAVE TO DO WITH YOU?

Let's go back to the rainy-day analogy. If they are in denial, and you come into the bedroom and state the fact that it's raining outside, and they argue it is sunny, their denial is easily overcome by lifting the window shade. They see what you see and admit to the fact that it is raining.

Conversely, when they are in delusion, and you are both looking out the same window, they don't see what you see. They have special glasses on which change what they see. The addict-alcoholic will confidently point out the window and say: "See? I told you it's sunny!" They are thoroughly convinced and it's their truth. You are left confused by how they could possibly say it's sunny when you are looking out the same window and it's clearly raining.

Self-delusion is pervasive and warps an addict-alcoholic's perception of everything concerning their using. They will defend themselves to you through those lenses of delusion. At times you might find yourself baffled at the ridiculousness of their excuses and reasoning. They don't seem to see what is right in front of them. You may think they are straight up lying and trying to gaslight you. In a delusion, they may not be trying to gaslight you; *they are simply defending the truth as they see it.*

Sometimes outside circumstances (such as getting fired from work or getting arrested) may help them to hit their "rock bottom" and smash their delusion. However, even with drastically bad situations, the fear of giving up their only tool for coping is so great they are blocked from being able to see the truth of what their substance abuse is doing to their life and to your relationship with them. When this is the case, it is virtually impossible for you to make them see the truth and help them.

When I was drinking, every now and then my partner would gently broach the topic of my drinking and the facts of what she saw. She was trying to help me. My response was to offer my (delusionary) counterpoint to what she was talking about. Almost always she would just drop the subject. In recovery, as we have had open conversations about what transpired during my active using years, she has shared with me that I caused her to doubt herself and her intuition. She lost touch with herself. I am very regretful I did this to the woman I love.

Being in a relationship with addict-alcoholics in delusion causes much frustration and heartbreak for people like you. The unconscious fear they have concerning giving up drugs and alcohol blinds them from recognizing a different way out from what they are doing. The best you can do is lovingly point out the facts as you see them. The purpose of sharing your truth is more for you to stand in your truth and stay connected to yourself rather than trying to convince your addicted loved one that "you are right."

Hopefully, in time, the addict-alcoholic will hit their "rock bottom," finally smashing their delusion and seeing their situation for what it is: that everything happening to them is because they are an addict-alcoholic. In the meantime, please don't let their delusion disconnect you from you. Stand in your truth…with love. Stick with your intuition and truth, and one day you might catch them at just the right time where they might finally see what you see.

3.6 WHY DO ADDICT-ALCOHOLICS USE?

It is taught in some recovery programs that addiction is a three-fold disease. Addiction is:

- in the body (physical),
- in the mind (mental/emotional), and
- in the soul (spiritual).

Physically

The addict-alcoholic's body becomes addicted. This is biology and means two things.

1. Physical cravings

For a physically addicted person, once even the smallest amount of alcohol or drugs is put into their body, it kicks off a physical compulsion to continue using at all costs. In recovery programs this is known as "the phenomenon of craving." The craving demands more drinking and drugging. I have heard countless stories of people who could not stop drinking or using until all the booze or drugs were gone or they were physically separated from drugs and alcohol.

For the addict-alcoholic, the bodily pathway of physical craving does not go away with an extended period of abstinence. The craving is just dormant because it's not being fed. It is so powerful that despite not using for years or decades, if an addict-alcoholic drinks or uses again, the cravings will drive many back into the throes of addiction within a short period of time.

In recovery meetings, there are two frequently mentioned quotes which describe the phenomenon of craving:

"It's the first drink that gets you drunk."

and

"The man takes a drink, the drink takes another drink, then the drink takes the man."

2. Withdrawal symptoms

Withdrawal symptoms happen when the body has become dependent on the use of drugs or alcohol, and the sudden absence of those chemicals causes a physical response (nausea, vomiting, inability to sleep, headaches, seizures, and severe anxiety or depression, to name a few). Withdrawal symptoms will be experienced if using is suddenly stopped.

Withdrawal symptoms are usually very uncomfortable and difficult to deal with. They can even be life threatening. Deep down, addict-alcoholics fear the process of withdrawal which drives them to keep using. It is important to seek out professional help (like a detox center) to manage withdrawal symptoms when getting physically sober. Detox centers monitor them and ensure their well-being during withdrawal.

Mentally and emotionally

Addict-alcoholics develop an obsession with using drugs or alcohol to change their mental and emotional state. When times are bad, using is to numb the pain. When times are good, using is to make the feeling even better. When times are indifferent, using is to make things more interesting. Chemicals become their only tool for coping.

This is how it works:

1. Uncomfortable emotions (which they may not be aware of) drive relief-seeking thoughts.
2. When the relief-seeking thoughts become repetitive, it creates an obsession with drinking and using drugs as a coping mechanism to find some peace, serenity and relaxation.
3. The obsession then causes thoughts about drugs and to run around their mind 24/7.
4. They use because of the obsessive thoughts.
5. Using then causes more negative emotions like guilt and shame, which then leads to more relief-seeking thoughts.
6. They use again because of the obsessive thoughts and the self-sustaining cycle continues to spiral downward.

The obsession is so strong that an addict-alcoholic will easily fabricate excuses to use. In short, no matter what the situation, they will find a reason to use.

They are frequently in a mental delusion that their using does not affect anybody around them, nor is it the cause of their life problems. Remember, a delusion means they believe their perception is true. The delusional mental mechanism helps them justify to themselves that drinking or drugging is not the root cause of their problems. This preserves their "right" to continue to use despite the obvious outside signs they are addicted.

The obsession (mental/emotional) combined with the phenomenon of craving (physical) means it is almost impossible for an alcoholic or addict to have "just one." Have you ever opened a bag of potato chips or your favorite snack and tried to have just one? If you found it difficult, you have felt a small fraction of what the addict-alcoholic experiences when they ingest chemicals. Perhaps you even found it difficult to stop eating until the bag was empty. Maybe you have experienced this with ice cream or chocolate. Perhaps you had a day where you were exhausted because you binge watched your favorite TV show late into the night before. If this is the case, you have experienced what it's like to have a craving. The addict-alcoholic's craving for chemicals is what you felt multiplied many times over.

Spiritually

From a spiritual angle, they break their own personal moral code of conduct time and time again. I have heard this said in story after story in recovery meetings: "I drew a line in the sand and told myself I would never do 'that' (intravenous drugs, steal, lie, drive drunk, etc. … fill in the blank), only to find myself over that line once again. So, I just drew a new line."

Check out this story from a good friend of mine (I will call him David) who has been sober almost 2 decades and now works a solid recovery program.

* * *

David's story of breaking his own moral code:

"At least I wasn't taking the 5's"

In my household growing up, I learned solid family values. My parents taught my sister and me to treat people with respect and to know the value of a dollar. With that foundation, both my sister and I got jobs very young and started to create our own savings. My older sister was a waitress at a restaurant and, at the age of 13, I had a job delivering newspapers to neighborhood households.

Despite growing up in a loving, supportive household, I had a huge self-confidence problem. I was constantly worried about what other people thought of me. I remember always feeling uncomfortable in my own skin. The palms of my hands constantly seemed to be sweaty.

Around the time I got my first job, the group of kids I hung out with started to drink alcohol and smoke pot. I was horrified, but I continued to hang out with them. Eventually I caved into peer pressure, and I tried drinking alcohol. I knew it was against the values my parents had instilled in me, but the feeling I got from drinking was profound.

For what seemed like the first time in my life I felt comfortable in my own skin, and my sweaty palms dried up. I justified the drinking by telling myself: "At least I am not smoking pot;

I will never do that." I had crossed my own boundary line of moral conduct, and my solution was to just draw a new one and tell myself I wouldn't cross it.

A year and a half later at the age of 15, I crossed the "no pot smoking" line, and I tried it. As with drinking alcohol, the feeling I got from smoking was profound. I felt like an equal to all my friends and I was the life of the party. Again, I knew smoking pot was not a good decision so I justified it to myself by thinking: "At least I am not smoking it every day; I will never do that." I drew another new boundary line. Guess what? Soon I crossed that line too and was smoking pot every day. I was chasing the feeling of peace I got from chemicals.

In less than a year, at the age of 16, I had spent all $3,000 of my savings on booze and pot. I was out of money, and a tremendous fear came over me. How was I going to get the feeling of peace? This is when I started seeking money from other sources.

One day as the fear took hold of me, this thought came into my head: My sister was getting cash tips from her waitressing job. I started searching her room for her tips. I distinctly remember the feeling I had. I knew it was wrong but this force within me pushed me to continue searching her room. Eventually I found a shoebox under her bed where she kept her cash tips.

The shoebox had a ton of change and paper bills. At that moment I thought: "There is no way she knows how much money is in here and if I just take a little change, she won't miss it." I knew what I was doing was wrong. As usual I had a sinking feeling in my stomach which I tried to ignore, so I justified my actions to myself: "At least I wasn't taking the ones." I drew another new boundary line.

She never said anything, so I convinced myself no harm was done. Eventually I coaxed myself into thinking it was OK to take the ones. I justified it to myself yet again: "At least I wasn't taking the 5's." Yep, another new boundary line. Guess what? I got bolder and eventually I moved on to the 5's, justifying it by telling myself: "At least I am not taking the 10's." Then it became the 10's and after that the 20's.

Each time I crossed a newly drawn line of moral conduct; the sinking feeling would return, and I would break out in a sweat. Knowing I would eventually be caught, I stopped taking my sister's money and moved on to other sources of stealing. One thing which helped me delude myself into thinking my actions weren't so bad was that all the friends I hung out with were doing much worse things than I was. I could point to them and say: "Well, at least I am not doing what they are doing."

Authors Note:

Notice how David's delusionary thinking extended to the words he used in telling his story. He used the phrase "taking the ones" instead of "stealing the ones." Taking and stealing are not interchangeable words! Taking is not necessarily stealing, but stealing is always stealing. His delusional thinking pushed him to use the word "taking" to lessen the severity of what he was doing in his own mind.

* * *

Spiritually, addict-alcoholics toss aside their personal morals and code of conduct if they get in the way of their using. They sometimes do terrible things.

A quote I hear often in recovery meetings is:

"When I used, all bets were off. I found myself in places I should not have been in, hanging around with people I should not have been with, doing things I should not have been doing."

Many times, the addict-alcoholic's actions end in humiliation, and deep down they frequently hate themselves for what their life has become. The personal loss of spiritual values is where addiction gets its moral stigma.

WHAT DOES THIS HAVE TO DO WITH YOU?

In the opening exercises in section 3.2, I asked you: "How would you personally define what an addict-alcoholic is?" My question for you now is: "How did your definition compare to what I just described in this section?"

As you frustratingly watch the addict-alcoholic make one bad decision after another, you may ask yourself, "Why do they continue to use drugs and alcohol?" The purpose here is to help you get a more complete picture of the answer to that question. The physical, mental/emotional, and spiritual aspects of addiction take control of their thinking. That thinking then drives behaviors which cause them problems in life. As the problems stack up, ironically addict-alcoholics reach even more to drugs and alcohol as the solution to these problems.

Addiction is a disease which affects the whole person - mind, body and spirit.

This is the downward spiral of addiction:

Using drugs and alcohol causes them problems, and ironically their perceived solution to those problems is to use even more.

Let's exemplify this through a scenario:

1. I have had a nagging feeling of discontentment in life. I am irritable all the time. As a result, I started drinking more to make those feelings go away.
2. My wife made a comment to me about how much I have been drinking and I lied to her about it. I told her I only drink once in a while when really, I am drinking at least four to five times a week.
3. I feel guilty lying to her, which makes me want to drink more to numb that out too.
4. After her comment to me, I must hide the drinking because I am afraid that she will call me out. Now I also feel ashamed that I am hiding my drinking.
5. I don't like feeling shame, so I need to drink even more now to get the same numbing effect.
6. Because I must hide it, I started drinking in my car on the way home from work. I ended up being pulled over by the police and I lost my license.
7. Now I feel humiliated because I got caught lying to my wife and I am embarrassed that she has to drive me to work.
8. Guess what I want to do now? You guessed it.....DRINK!
9. I feel so hopeless, I don't know what to do. I hate all these feelings which have built up from all these problems.

In the end, the addict-alcoholic becomes buried under a blizzard of negative emotions, making it very difficult to break the cycle. Because of addict-alcoholic delusion (discussed in the previous section, 3.5), they are unable to see that substance abuse is in reality the cause of their current life situation. I have heard active addict-alcoholics say: "You would drink too if you had my problems" … when drinking and drugging is the cause of their troubles in the first place!

Any situation or interaction which could prevent the addict-alcoholic from being able to drink or use feels suffocating and terrifying. When I was actively using, going on vacation was not relaxing, it was actually stressful! I didn't know how I was going to be able to drink the way I *needed to* while not getting in trouble with Nicole. Any situation like this will trigger fear and hence a fight-or-flight survival response in an addict-alcoholic.

The prospect of being denied drugs or alcohol ignites the primal fight-or- flight response in addicted loved ones.

The fight-or-flight survival response manifests as an overwhelming need to protect their ability to access and use drugs or alcohol. To accomplish this, the addict-alcoholic will do anything, even gaslight you. They will control and manipulate you in any way they must to enable using. Know that it is not personal to you; they will do it to anyone who gets in their way. It is not a moral issue, and they are not bad people. They are sick people with the disease of addiction.

The mental obsession and physical compulsion create irrational and insane thinking. The insane thinking creates decisions which break their own spiritual set of values. Their decisions are frequently baffling to people like you. You may try to apply logic to help them but because of their insane thinking, you may find it does not work.

At the end of the day, the addict-alcoholic's power in making good choices is given away to the disease of addiction. If you look at the first part of step 1 in Alcoholics Anonymous's (AA's) 12-step recovery program, it is:

"We admitted we were powerless over alcohol."

The addict-alcoholic is powerless over drugs and alcohol. This is true even when they want to stop using. I have heard countless stories of people who said they drank and drugged "without their own permission." To outsiders it may seem as though the addict-alcoholic is choosing their actions. Know that the addict-alcoholic is not freely choosing based on a sane mind; the disease of addiction is in control of their mind and in charge.

To summarize what all this has to do with you:

- Try not to take what they do personally, even though what they do may feel as if they are targeting you. They may lie, call you names, criticize you, blame you, and yell at you to get you to back off. Remember, their disease is in charge and what they do is all to defend their ability to use. It has nothing to do with how they really feel about you.

- The disease of addiction may drive them to do bad or "immoral" things. It is perfectly acceptable for you to hold them accountable for their actions.
- A quote I have heard for the loved ones like you is: "Hate the disease, not the person." Another way to say this is: "Our addicted loved ones HAVE a problem. They are not THE problem." This means do your best to support them with love while still keeping to your boundaries and holding them responsible for their behavior.

3.7 ADDICTION IS USUALLY NOT SUBSTANCE SPECIFIC

While most addict-alcoholics abuse multiple substances, almost all of them have their drink or drug of choice, their favorite. That substance is to their willpower as kryptonite is to Superman. When they finally admit they have a problem, many addict-alcoholics will confine the scope of their addiction to that kryptonite substance. They don't see that addiction most likely affects their relationship with all mind-altering substances. For example, I have heard addicts who will not identify as an alcoholic, the implied message being that they don't have a problem with, or abuse, alcohol.

In their mind they manufacture the delusion that their addiction is restricted to that one substance. This thought process is a protective mechanism which leaves the door open for them to potentially use other substances to cope with life while still being able to convince themselves they are sober. Remember a delusion means *they believe it.*

The disease of addiction could be described as *a tendency to abuse anything which helps them escape how they think and*

The disease of addiction could be described as *a tendency to abuse anything which helps them escape how they think and feel.*

feel. As we discussed in section 3.6 “Why do addict-alcoholics use?” the disease of addiction goes beyond just physical addiction. There are mental, emotional, and spiritual components to the disease. These threefold components mean that addicts have an affinity to lean on any chemical which affects their mental and emotional state. Deep down they hold the belief that substances are the solution to how they think and feel.

I have witnessed drug addicts say they were “clean,” yet they still would get drunk on alcohol. I have witnessed alcoholics say they were sober because they stopped drinking, yet they were still using marijuana. It is so common that there is a tongue-and-cheek term for this in the Alcoholics Anonymous community, it’s referred to as “California sober.” I did this myself, check out my own story about it.

* * *

My story of using marijuana when I first stopped drinking:

"My delusional thinking convinced me it was OK."

In the summer of 2014, after decades of abusing alcohol, I was really feeling the health effects. I had constant chest pains. Eventually, my chest pains got so bad I went to the hospital, where they found nothing wrong with my heart. I ended up surrendering to the fact that I was alcoholic and since that day in 2014 I have not had a drink.

Giving up drinking was my first huge step toward recovery. It was hard to do, and I had many fears concerning life without alcohol. Thoughts like "How am I ever going to have fun again?" swam around in my mind. I immediately started attending recovery meetings and got a "sponsor" very shortly after. With his guidance I started to work on the 12 Steps of Alcoholics Anonymous. I am forever grateful to him for all he did for me!

At the time I stopped drinking, I was also a heavy marijuana user, smoking all throughout the day. When I first stopped drinking, I was not ready to give up pot just yet, so I continued to smoke it. I went to a lot of recovery meetings early on, averaging one per day. At those recovery meetings, despite still using pot, I would declare myself "sober." As I hit monthly milestones for "sobriety," I proudly accepted the accolades from others in the meetings.

There was a gentleman I had met in recovery whom I was giving rides to meetings because he had lost his driver's license. One day about three months into my recovery journey, while we were in the car, he found out I was still smoking pot. Despite being a big burly guy, he said to me: "That makes me sad." He didn't yell at me, judge me, or guilt trip me. His emotionally vulnerable response really took me by surprise.

I asked why it made him sad. He said to me based on what he had seen and heard from me during my shares in the meetings, I really seemed to be doing great. And now comes the big BUT. He explained to me that although it was terrific I had stopped drinking, I was still using chemicals to cope with how I thought and felt, which is part of the definition of being an alcoholic or addict. Then came his unbridled honesty, a big blow to my ego. He said: "Basically, you are not sober."

This big burly guy telling me I wasn't sober in the way he did (with love) hit me like a ton of bricks. My delusional thinking up until that point had me convinced it was OK to still smoke pot. I really believed what I was saying when I declared myself sober at the recovery meetings. It took somebody besides myself, who I respected, to smash my delusion. For the first time I was able to see the whole truth in my situation; I wasn't sober just because I stopped drinking.

I finally told my sponsor I had been smoking pot while I had been working the 12 Steps with him. With love, he told me indeed I was not sober. He said some of the same things the other gentleman did, that I was still using chemicals as a crutch to cope with life. My sponsor had very solid moral values, and he told me if I did not get honest with myself and stop smoking pot, he could not sponsor me anymore. So, I finally quit marijuana.

Then came a big act of honesty and humility for me: I changed my sobriety date to the day I stopped smoking pot. I had to explain to all my new recovery friends why I was changing my sobriety date. The reaction I got was not guilt trips or judgments. It was love and support. I was amazed at the love shown by the recovery community around me. This truly put me on the path toward solid recovery. The experience also showed me how powerful delusional thinking can be, and how I needed close friends in recovery to help me out of it. My sponsor used to say to me: "Craig, you can't use the same brain that got you into this to get you out of it. You need people like me to help you see the errors in your thinking."

* * *

In recovery meetings I have heard many drug addicts say at the beginning of their story that alcohol was not a problem for them. Yet as they revealed further details, sticking a needle in their arm or smoking crack cocaine started with "having a few drinks" almost every time.

The fact is, it is rare to find a "pure" alcoholic or a "pure" drug addict who does not abuse any other substance. From some of the more honest (or non-delusionary) shares I have heard in recovery meetings, this quote comes up:

"My drug of choice was whatever I could get my hands on."

The key takeaways are:

- Having the disease of addiction means they will have the tendency to lean on subdtances to make themselves feel better mentally and emotionally (when they may not need them for health reasons).
- When somebody becomes addicted to any substance whatsoever, much of the time their general relationship with substances becomes changed and there is a high

probability they will abuse more than their "drug of choice."

Non-chemical targets may also emerge once they get physically sober. Some examples are:

- work
- eating
- social media
- shopping
- playing the lottery or gambling
- sex
- exercise
- any activity which causes a release of adrenaline or dopamine (they become adrenaline junkies)

Being addicted to other things like exercise or work is obviously not as bad as chemicals, but at what cost? The tendency of the addict-alcoholic is to feed the addiction, even when it is causing negative effects in their life. Overeating will eventually cause health problems. An over focus on sex can cause strain on their romantic relationships. We've all probably joked about "workaholics," but what do the long hours at work mean for the family at home? And what about adrenaline junkies who put their physical well-being at risk?

WHAT DOES THIS HAVE TO DO WITH YOU?

The addict-alcoholic in your life (especially in early sobriety) will sometimes think they were not, or won't become, addicted to substances besides their "drug of choice." *They might try to convince you of the same.* Remember if they are an addict-alcoholic, they will have a tendency to use substances to change how they think and feel instead of pursuing other more healthy coping mechanisms.

Even when they are abstinent from substances, you still may be affected by their disease. Sometimes the addict-alcoholic will shift their addiction onto non-chemical targets like work or exercise. There can certainly be a compromise with non-chemical targets, as many times addiction to those are not as disruptive to the household as abusing substances. I will call out two exceptions here: gambling and sex. Those two non-chemical targets can be very destructive.

When it comes to non-chemical targets for their addiction, it is for you to decide what's acceptable. How much is their focus on these other targets interfering with your relationship or the household? If things are better in general, and you are OK with it, then it is OK!

3.8 WHAT SUBSTANCES CAN BE ABUSED?

The general answer is: More than you realize! The website for the National Institute of Drug Abuse is a useful resource for a list and discussion. It may be found at www.drugabuse.gov/drug-topics. The addict-alcoholic can abuse a huge variety of prescription or even over-the-counter medications. I'm talking way more than your usual illegal drugs, prescription opiates, and alcohol. Some abusable substances come in sneaky forms which you may have never thought of such as baking extracts

Abusable substances come in many surprising forms.

(like vanilla extract) which have high alcohol content as the preservative.

Prescription medications

Prescription medications are obviously a huge target. Doctors certainly understand powerful opiate-based painkillers are a danger, and most are careful when prescribing them. What many doctors don't realize is that pain medications which advertise as non-addictive or non-drowsy can still be abused. I want to be clear: the doctors are not to blame; almost all of them are trying to be helpful. Many doctors simply don't realize the complete breadth and depth of addiction as a disease. It is the addict-alcoholic who is a master manipulator and knows how to report symptoms (they may or may not have) in a way which will get a desired prescription.

Some medications which advertise as non-habit forming, non-drowsy, or non-addictive can still be abused to get a high.

One other word on prescription medications. Sometimes addict-alcoholics need to be prescribed painkillers or other potentially high-inducing medications for heath conditions, surgery, or injury. Taking these is always a dangerous time for them because taking the medications may trigger their cravings. I have heard non-addicts say, "Well, just follow the instructions on the label and you will be fine." The problem is an addict-alcoholic may not be able to follow the instructions once they get the medication in their body. Their cravings may take over their thinking and away they go. In recovery meetings I have heard speakers lightheartedly talk about trying to follow prescription instructions this way:

"The label said take one pill every four hours and I read it as take four pills every one hour."

It's not just the doctors who put prescription medications in the hands of addict-alcoholics. The addict-alcoholic will look through other people's medicine cabinets for them. Over the years I have heard countless stories of people stealing medication while visiting an unsuspecting family member or friend. I did this myself when I was active. Just one or two pills here and there and nobody notices, right? If you live around an addict-alcoholic and have prescription medication, the only way to safely keep it is by locking it up in a secure place.

Check out my own story on this topic.

* * *

My own story about stealing medication:

"I was faced with admitting to it or lying to the police."

When I was still active, my mother-in-law lived in an apartment which was part of our house. One day she asked me to fix the sink in her bathroom. While I was there, I felt a pull to look through her medicine cabinet. I had never done anything like this before. I knew it was wrong, and I did it anyway.

I discovered she had many prescription medications in there. Upon inspection of the pill bottles, I noticed some of her medications had label warnings such as "do not operate heavy machinery while on this medication," or "may cause drowsiness," or "alcohol may intensify the effect." I took note of those particular medications.

When I was done fixing her sink, I went back to my side of the house and proceeded to look up those medications on the internet. I found websites which give specific instructions on how to get intoxicated off many of the medications she had: I discovered her medicine cabinet was a new source for a chemical buzz!

Over the next several months, when she went out, I would go next door and take some of the medication. I carefully noted where the pill bottles were, and how they were arranged. I only took a few pills at a time so she would not notice. When I was done taking the pills, I was careful to put the bottles in the same spots and to face labels the same direction they were before I touched them, again to avoid her detection.

At the time she did not notice what I was doing. The problem was I kept doing it. Over the course of months, I had stolen a lot of medication. One day she needed a medication she did not take frequently and noticed it was almost gone when it shouldn't have been. She inspected all her other bottles only to find many of them also depleted. She called my partner (her daughter) over and discussed what she had discovered. My mother-in-law did not suspect me and thought somebody had broken in and stolen her medication.

Intuitively, my wife just knew nobody had broken in. Her gut instinct told her it was me. She immediately came back and confronted me. I was horrified. So, I did what I always did to protect my use: I lied. My wife then said, "Well, if you didn't take them, then I have to call the police to report a burglary." She immediately took out her phone and started calling the police.

In the seconds that she was dialing the police, I had to decide: Do I tell my wife the truth or do I lie to her and the police? While calculating if I could get away with lying, I realized my fingerprints would be all over the pill bottles. I had no choice, the situation forced me to tell the truth. I felt incomprehensible humiliation in that moment; however, I did not stop drinking and drugging for another year.

Upon reflection from the sober place I am today, this was one of those instances which, although it seemed horrible at the time, now I am able to see it was one of the best things that ever happened to me. It turned out to be part of a string of events in my using which eventually led to hitting my rock bottom and seeking recovery. I will never forget the humiliation I felt in that moment when I got caught.

* * *

A few examples of prescription medications which you may not realize can and will be abused are:

- Painkillers which advertise as non-addictive, non-drowsy, or non-high inducing like gabapentin or tramadol. With these types of medications, don't trust what the manufacturer or doctor is telling you. Ask someone you know who is in recovery and they will tell you if you can get high off them!
- Anxiety medications: Many are benzodiazepines which act on the same receptors in the brain as alcohol and some drugs, so they are commonly abused by addict-alcoholics.
- ADHD medications are also a target because they are stimulants.

- Sleeping medication is also a frequent drug of abuse because with addiction comes sleeping problems (one of the most common withdrawal symptoms is the inability to sleep).

Over-the-counter medications (OTC)

Some OTC medications can be abused as well.

- Sleeping pills show up again as a target for the reason stated above: with addiction comes sleeping problems.
- Cough syrup containing dextromethorphan (DXM): DXM is the "DM" part you see on the label and is used as a cough suppressant. DXM is a powerful drug which induces intense psychedelic effects when abused.
- Motion sickness medications with the active drug dimenhydrinate (active ingredient in Dramamine) also induces powerful psychedelic-type effects when abused.

There is a plethora of OTC medications which can be abused beyond the ones listed above. The purpose of my discussion with you is not to list them all but to create awareness. Search engines on the internet make it incredibly easy for the addict-alcoholic to abuse anything which can induce a high. Instructions on how to get a buzz can be quickly found. Search results might be as simple as "take 4 of these and drink 3 beers and you will feel like this."

WHAT DOES THIS HAVE TO DO WITH YOU?

The list of abusable substances extends far beyond what you may think. Some of these items may be in your medicine cabinet right now. If you are not educated about what substances can be abused, you could be enabling the addict-alcoholic in your life. You might even be unknowingly supplying them with some of the substances they are abusing.

Don't believe the marketing from the makers of medications which claim the medication is "non-addictive" or that the medication cannot be used to get high. Doctors may not realize certain medications can be abused. If you are curious, look up the medications you have in your cabinet on the internet and find out from addict-alcoholics themselves if they are abusable. See if there is a "recipe" to get high from medications. If you discover some of your medications can be abused, safely lock them away. Look up the medications the addict-alcoholic has been prescribed or that they are getting over the counter. This will give you a more complete picture of what may be going on with the addict-alcoholic in your life.

3.9 ADDICT-ALCOHOLIC VERSUS PROBLEM DRINKER/USER

Here is a story from early in my recovery about the first time I heard the term *problem drinker.*

* * *

My story about hearing the term problem drinker for the first time:

"Problem drinker sounded much better than alcoholic to me."

For the last seven-ish years of my drinking and pot smoking, I knew I was leaning on it too much. I had the notion it was kind of a problem. I needed it to have fun. I needed it to cope with stress. I needed it to sleep. I knew I should stop at some point, but I wasn't planning on it anytime soon. I couldn't imagine actually giving it up or what the circumstances of stopping would look like.

Turns out I had a pretty shallow rock bottom (luckily for me and my family). I didn't lose my marriage, my house, or my job. I never lost my driver's license or got in trouble with the police. Actually, on the outside everything looked great. I had a beautiful wife, owned a house, and was killing it at my job. It was how I felt on the inside which drove me to my rock bottom and into recovery (the details of my rock bottom were in my story in chapter one).

In recovery meetings they would call me a "high bottom drunk." As an aside, I would like to tell you that just because I was a high bottom drunk, it doesn't mean my family did not feel the full emotional impact of living with me during my active years. Thank you to my lovely wife for sticking with me and walking with me on this journey of our healing.

Early in my sober journey, I went to a recovery meeting every day. I heard horrific story after horrific story of people burning their lives to the ground because of addiction. I began to question if I belonged in recovery. Was I really an alcoholic? Then I heard a term in a meeting which I latched onto: "problem drinkers." That sounded much better than "alcoholic" to me. Maybe I was just a problem drinker and user, which to me meant if I just worked out my problems, I could still drink and use.

I liked that thought. Not ever drinking or smoking pot again seemed a bit drastic to me…and overwhelming. So, it was a tough fork in the path. Do I take a left, admit I'm an alcoholic and never drink or use again? Or do I take a right, claim I was a problem user and attempt trying to maintain control once again?

Luckily, I expressed these thoughts and feelings in a recovery meeting and in turn received a great suggestion from a long-term sober person. His suggestion kept me going to recovery meetings long enough to learn the (sometimes subtle) differences between a problem drinker or user and an addict-alcoholic as well as where I was on that spectrum.

* * *

So, what is a problem drinker or user versus an addict-alcoholic?

It is common for non-addicts to situationally drink or use (certain) drugs to cope with big emotions such as grief, stress, sadness, or loneliness. The term for people like this is problem drinkers (or users). I want to be clear that when I use the term problem drinker (or user), my focus is that they drink or use heavily to cope with acute life problems. I do not mean that they have a problem with drinking or using, which they may or may not.

Unhealthy alcohol and substance use to deal with problems can range from mild to severe. Broadly speaking, it is my opinion that it's perfectly normal for people to utilize substances, temporarily, to help them through tough times. But where is the line between being a problem user and being an addict-alcoholic?

What I have come to find out is that there is no sharp defining boundary line. There is a gray area between the two which is challenging for a true addict-alcoholic. Why? Because with addiction comes addict-alcoholic delusion (as discussed in section 3.5 "Addict-alcoholics are not just in denial, they are also in a delusion"). Delusion means that the person maintains false beliefs. They unconsciously make up stories and facts to support their delusion. The important dynamic is they believe those made-up stories; it's their truth. In this case, the delusion is they are "not that bad"; they are just a "problem user" and not an "addict-alcoholic." That way, they preserve their right to drink and use.

OUTSIDE STRESSORS

Generally speaking, so-called problem users stop using heavily when the outside stressor is gone. The big stressful project at work finishes or enough time has passed that they heal from the emotional pain of a departed loved one. In the absence of the stressor, they find peace and stop abusing substances.

In contrast, addict-alcoholics continue to use heavily even after the stressor is gone or emotional pain has healed. In fact, the delusional thought process of addict-alcoholics will create a new stream of reasons to justify using. The reasons could be negative to try to make you feel bad for them, so you tolerate their using. The reasons can also be positive, such as, "It's time to celebrate! Join me!"

CONSEQUENCES

Problem users will stop using if there are consequences to their using, like being arrested for driving while under the influence or getting in trouble at work. Problem users typically learn from their mistakes and don't repeat them.

Addict-alcoholics will continue to use despite suffering numerous consequences. When consequences happen, addict-alcoholics just see them as a "bump in the road" or their delusion convinces them to blame the situation on someone or something else.

Addict-alcoholics can't control their disease (or disorder, whichever term you prefer) and typically repeat the behaviors which got them in trouble. Sometimes, to avoid getting in trouble the same ways again, addict-alcoholics will adjust when, what, or how they use. If a certain drug caused bad problems, maybe they stop using that drug. If they drank in the morning and got caught at work, then they wait until after work. The key is they keep using as much as they did before and eventually, they will get into different trouble.

CRAVINGS

Problem drinkers aren't so addicted that they can be a designated driver for a night and still have fun. If they are drinking at a party, they are able to just have one or two drinks without the craving to have more.

True "problem drinkers" (or users) can stop abusing substances, return to normal drinking *and be satisfied with it*. They haven't developed a physical or psychological dependance.

Once addict-alcoholics ingest even the tiniest amount of substances, they experience a craving for more. Because of the cravings, addict-alcoholics can't consistently just have one or two. If they start drinking, they typically continue until they get good and drunk (or until they pass out or black out). Addict-alcoholics rarely offer to be a designated driver because that means they can't drink the way they need to.

THE MENTAL OBSESSION

Problem users don't have a mental obsession with substances. They aren't constantly concerned whether there is "enough" booze or drugs.

Addict-alcoholics develop a mental obsession with substances which drives them to always plan to make sure there is "enough."

When you go to a gathering or on vacation with the addict-alcoholic in your life, do you think they bring more alcohol than what seems necessary?

Problem users don't have the mental obsession; they are not always thinking about drinking and using. They aren't constantly concerned whether there is "enough" booze or drugs. Addict-alcoholics' obsession drives them to think about drinking or using twenty-four hours a day, seven days a week. Even when they are not drinking and using, they are thinking about when they can. The mental obsession of addict-alcoholics drives them to constantly plan to make sure there is "enough."

Here is a story with another angle on the obsession and how strong mine was.

* * *

My story about the mental obsession:

"Even though I wasn't drinking, I was obsessed with how much my wife was."

Near the end of my active alcoholic days, my drinking was constant. I started in the morning, and drank all day, every day. I was getting into increasing trouble with Nicole. She constantly drove the two of us wherever we went because even though I hid my drinking from her, she didn't trust that I was in any condition to drive.

We had a date night planned for the weekend, and Nicole asked me if I wouldn't drink so that I could drive. She said she wanted a break from always driving us everywhere we went. On the outside I amiably said "sure," but on the inside I was NOT happy with this. Going out to dinner meant trying a great new beer or having some fancy cocktails (a lie I told myself and believed, when really, I just wanted to drink). I hid my dismay and agreed to be the designated driver.

Date night arrived and we were on our way to a Mexican restaurant, which of course had fabulous margheritas...that I couldn't have. Seemingly out of nowhere, I felt a bit of a bad mood coming on. We got to the restaurant, and there was a long wait for a table. I never usually minded long waits, because that meant I could have one or two drinks at the bar before we even got to our table, but not tonight. I still suggested we go to the bar so she could get a drink while we waited, but she declined. I said she should take full advantage of the fact that I was the designated driver. She wasn't persuaded, which annoyed me.

After about forty minutes, we were finally seated at our table. She of course ordered one of the fabulous margheritas with dinner. I stuck to my commitment and ordered a soda. As they do, the drinks came first. During our conversation while waiting for our food, I couldn't help but notice that she was barely touching her drink. This was really getting annoying. I mean, come on. When you have a designated driver it's a green light to get good and buzzed, right? Again, I pushed her to have more of her margherita, reminding her that she didn't have to drive home. Her response was: "I don't want to drink too much before our food comes because I will feel it." Now THAT was a foreign concept to me…I thought to myself, Isn't the point of drinking to feel it?

Our food came and as we ate, my mood continued to plummet. By the end of dinner, she hadn't even drunk half her margherita. I was getting snippy with her, and she asked me what was wrong. I claimed nothing, despite the fact that I was clearly being a jerk. Even though I wasn't drinking, I was obsessed with how much my wife was. Or, more accurately, how little she was drinking. It was incredibly frustrating for me to watch. By the time we got back in the car I was in a full-blown bad mood and the ride home was quiet. Fun date night, huh?

Today as I look back at that date night, I realize how much my obsession with alcohol took me over. Sure, I ruined things sometimes when I got drunk, but on that date night I ruined things because I wasn't drinking! My obsession with alcohol was constant. Every day of the week, morning, noon and night. Thinking, planning. Even keeping track of how much Nicole was drinking (or not drinking). I am so grateful I don't have that obsession anymore; it has completely left me from the work I have done in recovery, and it's a miracle!

REPEAT OFFENDERS

From my experience of going to thousands of recovery meetings, by the time a person has had enough of an issue to land them in rehab stints or recovery meetings, it is rare for them to be just a problem user. As we talked about, problem users stop abusing chemicals when the stress is gone. Problem users get in trouble once or twice, learn their lessen and stop. If someone has ended up in rehab or recovery meetings because of repeated and ongoing issues with substances, it usually has nothing to do with outside stressors or tough times. It is because they are an addict-alcoholic and using is their main tool for coping with life.

WHAT DOES THIS HAVE TO DO WITH YOU?

When an addict-alcoholic learns of the term problem drinker or user, they might latch onto it. They want to believe they are just problem users because that leaves the door open to still drink or use in some capacity. Once this line of thinking takes over, they may try to convince you they abused substances because they were just trying to cope with a tough time and that they are OK now. If they can convince you of this, deep down they know just maybe you will allow them to continue to drink or use without speaking up to them.

There are a few reasons addict-alcoholics latch onto the idea that maybe they are just a problem drinker or user:

- They feel shame, embarrassment, and fear the stigma which may come with admitting to being an addict-alcoholic, as discussed in the section 3.4 "The shame with the words addict and alcoholic."

- If they admit to being an addict-alcoholic, they know the most likely solution is abstinence, which causes tremendous fear and stress. The thought of abstaining from using for the rest of their life is overwhelming. So, if they can convince themselves they are only a problem drinker, it preserves their "right" to be able to still drink or use.

So, how do you know when the loved one in your life is truly an addict-alcoholic or just someone who is using to cope with a tough time? There is not an easy answer to this question. Defining what makes a person an alcoholic or addict is frequently not clear. There are online "quizzes" which serve as a guide to determine if there is a problem. I encourage you to do an internet search for "substance abuse quiz" which will yield many options for you to choose from.

Listen to what the online questionnaire says. Don't let the addict-alcoholic in your life try to convince you they are a problem drinker. You may not know the true answers to the questions as they are written for the addict-alcoholic; go through the questions anyway. It will help you get a more complete picture of some addict-alcoholic characteristics.

After all this discussion, know there are no hard boundaries between a *problem drinker (user)* and an *addict-alcoholic.* Between the two is a large spectrum of people who abuse substances. My intent in this section is to raise your awareness of the term problem drinker and how it pertains to the terms addict or alcoholic. One question I like to ask (which is really a question for the addict-alcoholic and not you the loved one) is this:

When they seem to control their drinking or using, are they satisfied with just having one or two?

For an addict-alcoholic, the answer to the question is no. I know this was true for me. If I was at a gathering (especially family ones) and I couldn't get drunk, I didn't bother having one or two like everyone else because for me that was just a tease.

In recovery meetings I have heard a funny phrase to describe addict-alcoholics who claim to be problem drinkers: "If it walks like a duck and quacks like a duck, it's a duck."

THE IMPLICATION OF MISDIAGNOSING

If your loved one is truly an addict-alcoholic, and they only admit to being a problem user and try to maintain control over drinking or using, at best it's a huge struggle. Before I got sober, I tried to moderate my drinking and using. Let me tell you, that was hell. Substances were my only tool for coping, and I didn't like how I felt when I wasn't drunk or high. Then, moderating my using and just getting "buzzed" didn't work. Drunk and high was my preferred destination and anything short of that was very frustrating. There is a story in the book *Alcoholics Anonymous* which has this tag line: "She finally realized that when she enjoyed her drinking, she couldn't control it, and when she controlled it, she couldn't enjoy it." This described me perfectly!

Because I wasn't getting enough substances in my system to cope with life, I was constantly irritable and a jerk to live with. I have heard many speakers at recovery meetings say that their loved ones told them, "I liked you better when you were drinking." This was true for me. In short, when I moderated, sure I wasn't drunk or high all the time, but my loved ones still suffered from my disease of addiction.

We have teased apart some differences between so-called problem drinkers and alcoholics; here are my final messages for you as their loved one:

- Ask your loved one to answer this question honestly for themselves: "When you have just a few, do you enjoy it, or do you find yourself wanting more?"
- You may not be able to figure out if they are a problem drinker or an alcoholic and that is OK. The important piece for you as the loved one is: if their drinking or using bothers you, then it bothers you. If it does bother you, tell them and stay true to yourself.

3.10 *PHYSICALLY ADDICTED* VERSUS *ADDICT-ALCOHOLIC*

Let's start with a short story about my mother.

* * *

My mother's story of being addicted, but not an addict:

"She was horrified at the fact that she was going through withdrawal!"

My mother, God rest her soul, was plagued with chronic back pain. With the close guidance of her doctor, she was prescribed opioid medications for decades to manage the pain. She seemed to always take them as prescribed, and we kids never noticed any signs that she was an addict. One time when she went on vacation with my oldest brother, she forgot her medication. She found herself not able to sleep, had general physical discomfort (in addition to the return of her back pain), and ended up having a bad case of diarrhea.

A few days into their vacation, my mother started complaining to my oldest brother Glenn about her symptoms, thinking she had contracted the flu or something. He was sober, well versed in addiction, and knew right away what was going on; she was going through opioid withdrawal. When he told her this, she was horrified at the fact that she was going through withdrawal because it begged the next question: Was she an addict herself? She certainly did not want to admit to that!

* * *

When Glenn told me this story, it sparked this discussion between us: "Can someone be addicted without being an addict-alcoholic?" We discussed the question for a while. With both my brother and I in recovery and having learned a ton, our answer is yes. People can become addicted without becoming an addict-alcoholic.

Here is why:

- When a medication is taken as directed, the medication and the body work together to heal. For some medications, when taken for a long period of time (even when you take the medication as directed) the body will become physically dependent on it. This is biology. The result is you will have withdrawal symptoms when you stop. If this happens, it does not mean you are an addict-alcoholic.

- In the same scenario, if the person is an addict-alcoholic, once they ingest the medication, they will experience physical cravings which drive them to use more. My mom did not appear to have cravings for more once she took the medication. She always took it as prescribed. She didn't mix it with alcohol like the label said. I know for me, when I saw "alcohol intensifies this effect" on a prescription label, that's exactly what I would do; drink to intensify the effect! So, my cravings pushed me to "intensify" the effect.
- As discussed in section 3.6 "Why do addict-alcoholics use?" addict-alcoholics also have a mental/emotional obsession.

My mom did not appear to have the mental/emotional obsession with the medication. My mother clearly did not have a mental obsession with her painkillers because she forgot to bring them on vacation! In her daily life outside of vacation, she wasn't constantly focused on when she last took it or when she could take it next. If she was under stress or feeling grief, she did not run to her pills to cope with those emotions.

- Also discussed in 3.6 is that addict-alcoholics exhibit a spiritual loss of values.

My mom did not demonstrate a spiritual loss of values. She didn't lie about her medication. She didn't lie about how much she was taking. She didn't lie to her doctor to get more. She didn't try to find another source to get more than what her doctor had prescribed. Taking her medication did not interfere with her ability to take care of life obligations. She did not manipulate her loved ones to maintain her ability to use.

WHAT DOES THIS HAVE TO DO WITH YOU?

When somebody is physically addicted to a substance, they will experience a period of withdrawal after stopping. If it is only physical addiction, after the withdrawal they return to their normal self.

When somebody is an addict-alcoholic, there is more to addiction than just becoming physically dependent. Almost all addict-alcoholics and their loved ones (people like you) don't know the disease of addiction goes way beyond just being physically addicted.

I have heard about many addict-alcoholics who got "dry" and then became miserable to live with. "Dry" means they got physically sober but did not work on the mental/emotional and spiritual facets of the disease. When addict-alcoholics give up their only tool for coping (chemicals), and don't work on the mental/emotional and spiritual facets of the disease, they have a tough time coping with life. Addict-alcoholics need to rewire their thinking and emotional responses when they stop drinking or using. Good recovery programs address all three facets of the disease.

> Just because someone becomes physically addicted, it does not mean they are an addict-alcoholic.

While the rewiring is happening, you may still be affected by their disease. They might be short tempered, generally irritable, or anxious. Remember the quote from the loved ones I had in the previous section: "I liked you better when you were drinking." If you have ever felt this way you are not alone!

3.11 SMASHING THE STEREOTYPE: THE MANY FLAVORS OF ADDICT-ALCOHOLICS

This topic is all about stereotypes and how they can hinder a person's ability to admit they are an addict-alcoholic. Here's my story.

* * *

My story about comparing myself to stereotypes:

"I had the belief that if I just used on the weekends, then I wasn't an addict or alcoholic."

I hit the height of my active addiction in my mid-thirties. At that time, I did not think the words alcoholic or addict applied to me despite drinking twelve to fifteen beers every day and smoking pot every few hours. After all, I was married to a smart and beautiful woman, owned a gorgeous house with a three-car garage, a car which I fully paid for, a vintage VW for fun, and was hugely successful at my job. I was what you would call a "highly functional" addict-alcoholic.

Then as I eventually got busted by Nicole over and over, things came to a head. I had to admit to myself that drinking and using every day is certainly a sign of an addict-alcoholic... so my solution was to cut back and just drink on the weekends.

That way I could prove the labels addict or alcoholic did not apply to me. So, I became a "weekend warrior" when it came to drinking and smoking pot.

I also cut back the amount I consumed. I was trying to moderate the "how often" and the "how much." On the surface, at first, I appeared successful. The thing is, this is what was going on in my head:

- *During the week I was constantly thinking about Friday when I could drink and smoke pot again. I had obsessive thoughts about alcohol and drugs. I've since learned in recovery there is a term for this, it's called "white knuckling" it. I was holding on with all my might during the week, waiting for the weekend.*
- *Cutting back on the amount when I "allowed" myself to drink and smoke was simply not satisfying...as a matter of fact it was frustrating. Once I started, I craved the feeling of being drunk and high, so the business of moderating the amount was just a tease.*
- *I became irritable all the time because I wasn't getting enough of my only tool for coping: substances.*
- *I had the belief that if I just used on the weekends, then I wasn't an "addict" or "alcoholic."*

Turns out I was wrong, that "weekend warriors" can also be addict-alcoholics.

* * *

The classic Hollywood stereotype of an addict-alcoholic is a dirty, trench coat-wearing, homeless person who drinks from a bottle in a brown paper bag. For many addict-alcoholics (like me!) and loved ones like you, this picture is frequently a measuring stick used to identify alcoholism or addiction. I want to tell you from my personal history and the thousands of stories I have heard in over ten years of recovery that the Hollywood stereotype as a measuring stick is doing nobody any favors.

A common reaction I hear from new people who come into recovery meetings for the first time is this:

"But I can't be an addict or alcoholic! I have a successful career, I pay my bills, and I'm still married!"

The fact is, the way addiction manifests in someone's life has an infinite number of possibilities. Most of the time the signs of addiction do not match the classic checklist of being unemployable, having gin blossoms all over their face, being homeless, being penniless, being a barfly, or being an absentee parent. Many addict-alcoholics don't even come close to checking any of those boxes. The fallacies of what an addict-alcoholic looks like make it challenging for the addict-alcoholic and their loved ones to accept the truth that full-fledged addiction may be present. Shame also interferes with the ability to accept the situation for what it is, as discussed in 3.4 "The shame with the words addict or alcoholic."

Can you relate with any of the thought bubbles that follow?

Accepting that a family member or friend is an addict-alcoholic can be tough. It is human nature to discount a serious situation based on the absence of the typical addict-alcoholic stereotypes. Many addict-alcoholics never lose a job or get arrested.

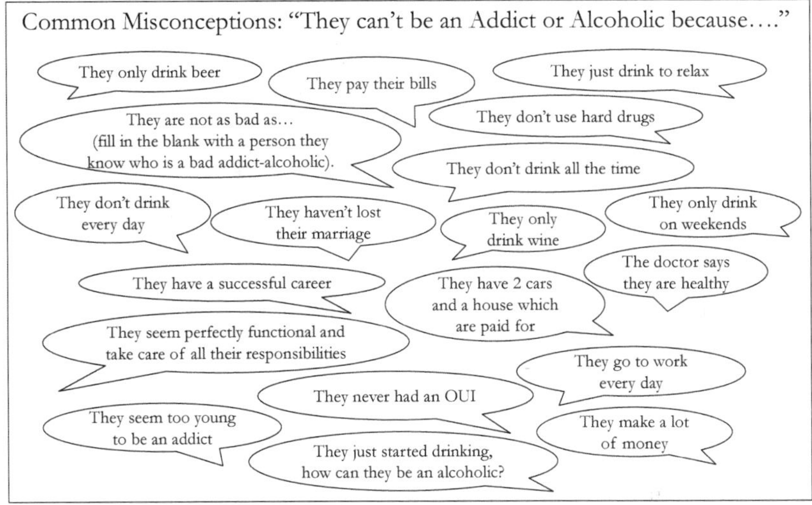

The truth is the extreme case of a homeless drunk or junkie who has lost everything is a small percentage of the actively addicted population. I have seen top-level corporate executives walk through the door of a recovery meeting looking completely demoralized. In my experience, most addict-alcoholics exist in the vast continuum between the skid row drunk and the top-level executive. In some cases, it is easy to see that a person has a substance abuse problem. In other cases, you may be shocked to hear someone you know well tell you they have a substance abuse issue. From the outside looking in, many times they appear to be regular, everyday people.

When I finally accepted my situation, got sober and told my dad I was an addict-alcoholic, he was absolutely shocked. At the time my dad had been sober for twenty-eight years and was fully entrenched in recovery. He helped so many people that when he passed away (of old age), his core recovery group named their meeting room after him. Why was he so surprised by my situation even though he had literally decades of experience working with alcoholics? It's because I was an expert hider and didn't display any of the stereotypical signs of addiction.

WHAT DOES THIS HAVE TO DO WITH YOU?

The point of this discussion is to emphasize that a person does not have to burn their life to the ground to be an addict-alcoholic. There are millions of so-called "functional" addict-alcoholics. Despite being in the grip of active addiction, these people maintain a marriage, a job (sometimes very successfully), and all the other responsibilities which come with life.

There is not a one-size-fits-all definition or description of an addict-alcoholic.

If you confront your potentially addicted loved one, they may try to convince you they are not an addict-alcoholic. You may recognize some of their reasons straight from the misconceptions shown in the thought bubbles above. At times you may have even convinced yourself they are not an addict-alcoholic for those same reasons.

This absolutely happened between Nicole and me. Once I finally accepted that I was an addict-alcoholic, and had real, truthful conversations with her about it, she told me all along her gut was telling her that I had a serious problem. However, because I was an expert hider and "high functioning" (I didn't match the addict-alcoholic stereotypes), it took away her confidence to approach me about it. Sometimes she would get the strength to ask me about my drinking, and I would cite some of those things in the thought bubbles to defend myself and prove there wasn't a problem.

Although she would drop the subject in the moment, she told me after I got sober that her intuition still told her I was an addict-alcoholic. So, during my active years, she developed this internal conflict between her logical brain (influenced by me and my manipulation) and her intuition. This is how she became sick too.

Whatever you may be witnessing from your potentially addicted loved one, you are probably only seeing the "tip of the iceberg."

Throw away the common misconceptions of addict-alcoholics you may have in your mind. In section 3.9 "Addict-alcoholic versus problem drinker/user" I referred to online "quizzes" for whether someone in your life may be an addict-alcoholic. Although the quizzes are for them to take, the questions also help you gain a better understanding of the signs of addiction.

Keep in mind that if the person you may be worried about is truly an addict-alcoholic, then they are most likely hiding a lot from you, even if it's your life partner or child. Whatever you may be witnessing from your potentially addicted loved one, you are probably only seeing the "tip of the iceberg."

3.12 ONCE AN ADDICT-ALCOHOLIC, IS IT FOREVER?

This is a hot-topic question for a few reasons.

1. The thought of "forever" is overwhelming for an addict-alcoholic trying sobriety for the first time.

2. There is debate among some people as to whether someone can eventually return to "normal" drinking.

The thought of "forever" can be overwhelming

When an addict-alcoholic is trying out recovery meetings for the first time, they may hear members say that indeed once a person is an addict-alcoholic, it is forever. I have heard this saying in many recovery meetings:

"Once you become a pickle, you can't go back to a cucumber."

"Forever" can certainly be overwhelming. Thoughts about all the activities they do which involve drinking swim around in their mind. They may think things like, "You are telling me I can never have a glass of wine with dinner, or a beer at the baseball game ever again?!" Those types of thoughts are common and are totally normal.

For people who use drugs and alcohol as much as addict-alcoholics do, it's hard for them to imagine the remainder of their life without drinking or using. I have personally seen how overwhelming this concept is for new people in recovery. For some of them, they just give up on recovery because forever makes them feel like *why even try.*

This is where the Alcoholics Anonymous concept of "one day at a time" comes from. Break it down into bite-sized pieces that are much easier to digest.

The debate of whether an addict-alcoholic can return to "normal" drinking or using

Now onto the real debate. Is it forever?

In section 3.6 "Why do addict-alcoholics use?" we talked about the physical cravings and the mental obsessions addict-alcoholics develop with substances. It is not debatable that cravings and obsession occur with addict-alcoholics. If you go to recovery meetings and listen to speakers you will hear this over and over.

Why am I talking about cravings and obsession when the topic of this section is whether someone is an addict-alcoholic forever? If someone has been sober for some period of time, and they want to test whether or not they are still an addict-alcoholic, the only way to do that is drink or use and see what happens. The risk? Their cravings kick in and BAM! They are in a tailspin of addiction once again. How long will it last this time? One week, one month, years, decades? Some relapses end with the person dead. I have personally sponsored people who used again and died as a result.

In my opinion, the question of "Is it forever?" is the wrong question to debate. I believe the debate should focus on this topic instead:

Testing to see if they are "cured" is DANGEROUS; is it worth the risk?

My experience from watching others

I have not personally tested out this theory of being "cured." I have not had a sip of alcohol or smoked pot since I got sober. In short, I have not relapsed. I have discovered from the thousands of recovery meetings I have gone to that I am in a very small minority. So, I will share my experience from watching others in recovery for over ten years.

In my estimation, testing out whether the person is "cured" will simply end up in a relapse. What I have witnessed is once somebody becomes an addict-alcoholic, their physical and emotional relationship with substances is forever changed. It is like a relationship gone sour. Once a relationship degrades to constant fighting and despising each other, it is impossible to go back to the magic of the first date.

There are always exceptions to the rule, so I won't say that 100% of people will be an addict-alcoholic forever. I concede that it might be, and I stress *might be*, possible for someone who became an addict-alcoholic to return to normal drinking or using some day. In my opinion it would take an exceptional, spiritually advanced person to completely reset their relationship with substances. *If this were to be possible,* the percentage of people who get to this space would be very low compared to the ones who just trigger another round of relapse which could last years or decades. In my greater than ten years' experience, I have yet to meet a true addict-alcoholic who was able to go back to normal drinking. By normal drinking I mean can they answer yes to these two questions:

1. *Are they able to effortlessly maintain a "normal" level of drinking or using over the long term?*
2. *Are they satisfied with drinking or using "normally"?*

What I have heard from people who have tried using again

Many people have shared in recovery meetings that after years of sobriety, they lost touch with how bad things were when they first got sober. Their memory of the situation they were in years before had softened over time. In short, they thought perhaps they overreacted.

I have also heard stories where addict-alcoholics falsely believed their long period of abstinence "cured" them. So, what happened when this delusional thinking crept in? They tried drinking or using again. Then, that one drink or drug in their system kicked in the physical cravings just like it did years or decades before. Most of these types of stories reveal that in a relatively short amount of time, they ended up right back where they were before they got sober.

For some addict-alcoholics, if they try drinking or using again, it only takes days to end up right back where they were before they got sober. For others it may take weeks or months. If there isn't an immediate downward spiral, it supports their delusion that they are OK to drink or use again, but eventually the physical cravings and mental obsessions take over.

So, at the end of the day, yes it *might* (again I emphasize might) be possible there is a very small percentage of people who can transcend addiction and completely reset their physical and emotional relationship with substances. But what happens to the vast percentage of addict-alcoholics when they test to see if they have been "cured"? Broken lives once again, that's what happens. So, is it worth the risk to test "Is it forever"?

Addiction is an illness where it is rare for the afflicted person to regain the ability to drink or use normally again.

WHAT DOES THIS HAVE TO DO WITH YOU?

The addict-alcoholic may try to convince you they overreacted or were "cured." Remember, they may be in a delusion; they believe what they are saying. They may say something like, "I had an issue a long time ago, I had a lot of stuff going on and that's why I got in trouble with using. I'm different now."

I experienced this scenario with my oldest brother Glenn; here's the story.

* * *

My brother Glenn convinced me he could drink again:

"Meh, that problem was a long time ago."

By the time I was in my twenties, I knew my brother Glenn had some struggles with substance abuse problems. The thing is, my family never talked openly about anything sensitive, so I didn't know the extent of his problem. I also had very little, if any, real knowledge about the disease of addiction. What I did know was my brother had abstained from alcohol for years.

One time he took me to a hockey game. I remember he went to the concessions stand and when he came back, he had a beer in his hand. I mustered up the courage to question him about it, and his response was, "Meh, that was a long time ago."

It was a nondescript comment; he didn't claim he was cured or that he overreacted. He simply let it hang out there that "it" (his drinking alcoholically) was a long time ago. Even though I felt in my gut there wasn't something right about his rationale, it worked on me because I dropped the subject. At the time I didn't know any better. Drinking a few beers at the game turned out to be the beginning of another downward spiral for him.

* * *

One key point to my story is my family never talked about these types of things, so I had no idea the seriousness of what I was witnessing at the hockey game. Now you know they do not become cured of the physical cravings which occur once they ingest substances. For most addict-alcoholics, drinking/using leads to more drinking/using. If you find yourself in a similar situation, simply state you have read up on this and once somebody becomes an addict-alcoholic, there is a high probability it is not safe for them to drink or use ever again. Talk openly about it, with love, and you will do your part to not participate in their active addiction.

3.13 WHAT DO ADDICT-ALCOHOLICS FEEL ABOUT THEIR SITUATION?

Addict-alcoholics usually have some kind of discontentment with life. A common one I hear is that people (especially younger ones) have insecurity and a desire to fit in. So, they drink or use to "loosen up." Other times the discontentment manifests as restlessness, irritability, or depression. So, they drink or use drugs to feel some peace. In turn the drinking and using causes them to become surrounded by more problems, reinforcing their discontentment. The problems could be at work, with their health, with their relationships, with the law, or with money. Because of their delusion, which we talked about in section 3.5, many times they are unable to accept that their problems all have the same root cause: their drinking and using.

The delusion will push them to blame their problems on anything but their substance abuse. They have problems at work because their boss or colleagues are jerks, their health issues are an unfortunate result of their inherited genes, their troubled relationships are because the other person is unreasonable, the police are treating them unfairly, etc. In short, they think they are a victim of outside circumstances.

Let me share a quick story about how I dealt with a health situation.

* * *

My story about blaming the health effects of drinking on something else:

"I cheated on my blood test!"

In the last few years of my drinking and using, I was approaching forty years old. Nicole and I decided to start trying for children. I hadn't been to a yearly physical with my doctor in well over a decade. Nicole convinced me I should get a checkup, so I did.

The physical included getting a blood test. In the appointment, the doctor reviewed my blood test results and it turned out I had a few items which were out of range. We discussed why they may have been out of range. She asked me about my alcohol consumption, and I lied to her. I told her I was drinking maybe four drinks a week when really, I was drinking more than twelve drinks every day. Because I lied, the doctor did not show any concern for the out-of-range results. With the misinformation I fed her, we looked at other reasons why, for example, my triglycerides were very high. I admitted I ate ice cream every night after dinner. So, I latched onto the ice cream as the reason for my high triglycerides.

When I got home from the appointment Nicole asked me how it went. Giving her the least amount of information possible, I replied, "It went fine, no issues." She asked to look at my blood test results.

Nicole immediately opened her computer and proceeded to use search engines to look at the top causes of why certain items on my blood test were out of range. Guess what? Every one of them came back with excessive alcohol consumption as one of the top reasons. I was horrified! I stuck to the ice cream story saying, "It must be because of all the ice cream I'm eating." I told her I would not eat ice cream anymore and to see how that went.

A year went by, and it was again time for my annual check-up. Deep down I knew my out-of-range blood test results from the year before were from my drinking. My solution to this was to dial back my drinking two weeks prior to getting my blood pulled for the test. Basically, I cheated on my blood test! As expected, the test came back with everything within range. When I returned home, I happily handed the blood test results over to Nicole, like an elementary school kid who just got a 100 on a spelling quiz. I used the current blood test results to convince her my previous year's out-of-range results were indeed from the ice cream.

* * *

WHAT DOES THIS HAVE TO DO WITH YOU?

Addict-alcoholics will tease apart all their problems as separate issues with separate causes. That way, it's difficult for people like you to group their problems together, connect the dots and realize the problems are all caused by their drinking and using.

Blaming a bunch of different outside circumstances for their predicament makes them a victim. If they can convince themselves they are a victim, then they are not responsible for their problems. When they convince you they are a victim, maybe you will feel bad for them and tolerate their drinking and using.

If you hear them blaming other people/circumstances or making a statement like "Why is this happening to me?" it should be a huge red flag to you that they are claiming victim status and not owning responsibility for their situation.

3.14 HOW DO ADDICT-ALCOHOLICS FEEL ABOUT THEMSELVES?

Almost all addict-alcoholics have tremendous inner turmoil. They want to stop drinking or using and they can't seem to. Conscious awareness of their sometimes bad behavior periodically penetrates their delusions. Every now and then, they do recognize deep down that some things they do are not good for them. They may even have some awareness that some things they do are morally wrong. The addiction-driven behaviors do not represent their true selves, and this is where the inner turmoil comes from.

Over time they feel as though they are a moral failure and are weak in character. I hear over and over from addict-alcoholic's stories how they absolutely loathed themselves. With that comes more shame and self-pity. The ironic thing is their solution to these bad feelings is to use more. After all, the number one coping mechanism for an addict-alcoholic is to numb themselves with substances (despite the problems being caused by using in the first place!).

So, seeking relief their thoughts go to drinking or using, as more drugs and alcohol are used, the bad behavior continues, the feelings get even worse, then they use more to cope. This is the downward spiral of the disease of addiction.

Check out this story from one of my close friends in recovery (I will call him Steven).

* * *

Steven's story about self-image:

"My 'a-ha' moment when I accepted that addiction was not a moral failing."

I was a really bad alcoholic, drinking every day all day. I just couldn't stop. When I finally agreed to go to a 28-day rehabilitation program, I felt completely demoralized and horrified at what I had become. In rehab they taught us how addiction was a disease. Despite having that knowledge, I still felt tremendous shame and self-loathing in my heart. I thought I had addiction problems simply because I was a loser.

This all turned around one day when my wife came to visit me. I was beating myself up in front of her. I was revisiting all the bad things I had done to her and the kids, such as stealing money from our own daughter. I was making my emotional state worse and worse.

After my wife listened to me for a while, she finally said, "Honey, stop beating yourself up. Addiction is recognized as a disease. It's not a moral issue. Your health insurance is even paying for you to be in this rehab, so they see it as a disease as well!" Her statement about my health insurance paying for rehab really hit home for me.

This was the turning point where I began to understand with my heart instead of my head that addiction was indeed a disease. It was my "a-ha" moment when I accepted addiction was not a moral failing. I finally started to accept I wasn't a bad person for abusing substances and doing the bad things I did. The shame, self-loathing, and self-pity started to melt away. The endless mental and emotional loop of revisiting all the bad things I had done and feeling self-pity stopped. I was free from the weight of those heavy, self-imposed emotions for the first time in a very long time.

This moment turned out to be the beginning of my journey into recovery.

* * *

WHAT DOES THIS HAVE TO DO WITH YOU?

There are times when the addict-alcoholic in your life may not seem to care about the damage they are doing or the hurt they are causing (to themselves and you). As bad as their situation looks on the outside, that is how bad they feel on the inside—or maybe even worse.

Know that when the addict-alcoholic in your life goes down the emotional spiral of shame, self-pity, and self-loathing, it frequently increases their desire to use. These negative emotions are usually a huge barrier to recovery for them. They want relief from the negative feelings, and drinking or using is the only way they seek relief. Then they use again and feel even worse.

When you see them in this state you might feel sympathy for them because you love them. The key point for you is not to let your sympathy interfere with defending your boundaries. Addict-alcoholics know if they are able to get sympathy from you, maybe you will let them drink or use without hassling them. Just because they feel shame, self-pity, or self-loathing does not mean it is OK for them to use. These are the things you can do with love:

- Remind them addiction is a disease, not a moral or character failing.
- Gently state using is what is causing these problems in the first place so using more will only make things worse.
- Continue to love them.

What they do with what you say is up to them; you have no control over it. All you can do is state your position (again with love) and defend your boundaries.

3.15 WHAT IS "HITTING ROCK BOTTOM"?

I had some pretty low moments during my active drinking and using years. I experienced the humiliations of getting caught sneaking drinks, my wife finding drugs in the pockets of my jeans, and not remembering what happened the night before—all the usual stuff an addict-alcoholic goes through.

Toward the end of my active time, there was one particular incident which was especially low. It was the story I shared about stealing medications from my mother-in-law in section 3.8 "What substances can be abused?" I can't tell you enough how humiliating it was when I was caught. When Nicole threatened to call the police, my humiliation was so strong I even considered lying to the police! But guess what? That wasn't my "rock bottom." I drank and used for another year until I hit my personal rock bottom.

The addict-alcoholic's continued abuse of substances despite their world collapsing all around them is heartbreaking and baffling for people like you. The friends and family simply do not understand why the addict-alcoholic keeps causing so many problems for themselves. As you watch them suffer so many consequences from their using, it seems like it should be enough for them to want sobriety, right? Unfortunately, most of the time it's not the case. Addicts and alcoholics must personally hit rock bottom to want recovery.

Can you relate to any of the quotes below I have heard muttered by many family members and loved ones?

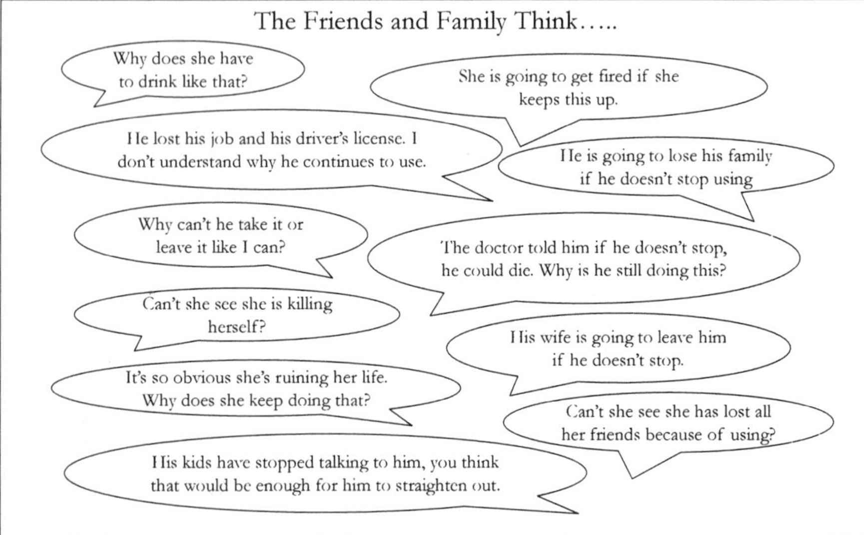

So, what is hitting rock bottom?

It is hard to define, and it is different for every addict-alcoholic. This is my own working definition for our discussion purposes:

> **Rock Bottom: The pivotal point at which a person finally accepts in their heart that they can't live the way they are anymore, *and they take action to change.***

In the moment of their personal rock bottom, they finally admit to themselves they just can't live the way they are anymore. They experience such an emotional breakdown that their delusions are smashed. The emotional pain finally drives them to *take action* to get sober. They may experience a deep mental and emotional change, a sort of "awakening." Someone who has hit rock bottom exhibits a few of these characteristics:

- Their emotional pain is so overwhelming that they cannot ignore it, and substances don't numb the pain like they used to.
- The protective armor of their delusionary thinking has been penetrated. They start to see the situation for what it truly is.
- They finally accept in their heart they have the disease of addiction, *and they admit it.*
- They start to become open to suggestions. They realize they probably can't get sober on their own and they accept help. This could be in the form of going to recovery meetings, going to detox, or going to a 28-day rehab program.

The heartbreaking truth for people like you is that there might be very little you can do to make the addict-alcoholic in your life "see the light" and straighten out for good. They must hit their rock bottom to finally change. It may not matter if you carefully choose the words, perfectly choose the timing, or get friends and family together for an intervention.

Rock bottom is different for everyone. Some hit it after a minor incident, while others must burn their life to the ground to get to rock bottom.

This is not to say you should not do an intervention. Interventions from people like you are sometimes a powerful emotional experience for the addict-alcoholic. Many begin their journey of recovery based on interventions. Know that recovery centers frequently have professionals who moderate interventions. If you want to have an intervention, I recommend contacting a few recovery centers near you to see what kind of support they offer.

Hitting rock bottom is a process, not an event

Hitting rock bottom is a process which involves experiencing many "smaller" bottoms along the way. The tough part for you is for years or even decades you may have watched your addicted loved one:

- cycle in and out of physical sobriety,
- get fired from one or more jobs,
- total their car,
- ruin their relationships,

- end up in jail, or
- end up in the hospital or even almost die because of using.

Hitting "a bottom" versus "rock bottom"

Just when *you think* they have reached rock bottom, the addict-alcoholic uses again and makes everything even worse. Here's the thing: It doesn't matter what you think. Remember they are in a delusion. Even though you see they are ruining their life, for them to change *they must perceive and accept it for themselves followed by the resolve they just can't live that way anymore.* Like an elevator which never seems to stop going down, watching their descent toward rock bottom is both frustrating and gut-wrenching.

Chances are, you and your addicted loved one have a very different idea of "rock bottom."

When they experience humiliations and consequences like those listed above, it might spark some desire to change in them, but not enough to really gain a solid resolve to change for good. The addict-alcoholic may even admit they hit a bottom. Your hopes soar when you witness this. Despite gaining some physical sobriety, deep down, most addict-alcoholics will still hold onto the idea that substances are the solution to their problems. Then, at some point, days, weeks, or months down the line, they show up drunk or high again. What happened? They hit "a bottom" but not "rock bottom."

Remember, they are in a delusion. Even though you see drinking and drugging is ruining their life, they don't see it.

Their addict-alcoholic delusions concerning the role of chemicals in their life must be smashed.

Their cycles of hitting a bottom followed by using again drags people like you into the emotional roller coaster ride of addiction. It's painful to be a part of and you may feel helpless. When they use again your optimistic hopes become crushed. You might get very angry with them.

Their struggle becomes your struggle. This is one reason why addiction is called a "family disease."

After that incident I had with stealing my mother-in-law's pills, my wife was both angry at me and sad for me at the same time (two conflicting emotions). She undoubtedly got sucked into my disease and became collateral damage to my addiction.

Rock bottom looks different for all addict-alcoholics. Some hit their rock bottom after just a few bad consequences, while others continue using for decades and must completely burn their life to the ground. For me, it was no specific incident; it was the cumulative effect of many little bottoms along the way (like the incident of stealing pills from my mother-in-law) which finally penetrated my armor of delusion and brought me to the last day I drank and used. More on that below...

"OUTSIDE" VERSUS "INSIDE" BOTTOMS

So, what does it take for an addict-alcoholic to hit rock bottom? It could be some of those things listed earlier in this section like an arrest, divorce, or being fired from work. In recovery meetings, we call those "outside bottoms." We also discuss another type of bottom: "inside bottoms."

Outside bottoms:

- These are incidents such as the loss of a job, marriage, relationship, house, driver's license, an overdose or using-related health problems (like liver problems).
- For the family and friends, outside bottoms seem as though they should be enough to drive anyone to seek sobriety. The quote bubbles in the diagram near the beginning of this section are loved ones' responses to witnessing outside bottoms.
- For an addict-alcoholic, even very serious outside bottoms may not be enough to spark a deep mental and emotional "awakening" for it to be their rock bottom.

Inside bottoms:

- These happen when they experience such tremendous emotional pain that they realize and accept they just can't live the way they are anymore. Inside bottoms may happen at any time and are not necessarily caused by a specific incident from their drinking and drugging.
- It is an "awakening" where their thought processes begin to rearrange, and their delusions become smashed. Abandoning their delusions is the beginning of deep mental and emotional change.
- It may take numerous inside bottoms to hit rock bottom. They may hit an inside bottom, and you hear them make statements with 100% conviction they are done drink-

ing or drugging, only to witness a fall soon thereafter (sometimes the same day).

- Only time will tell if their new inner resolve proves to be a temporary or permanent change of behavior.

Typically, it takes many outside bottoms to push an addict-alcoholic to arrive at an inside bottom. I am talking *a lot* of outside bottoms: sometimes dozens and even hundreds. Their delusional thinking is so powerful they can attribute outside bottoms to any cause except using. I have some friends in recovery who have gone to detox more than twenty times! The key to the start of their recovery was they hit an inside rock bottom.

My story in chapter one revealed my inside rock bottom. My outside bottom was the scare of potentially having a heart attack. I knew deep down the chest pains I was experiencing had something to do with my drinking and that fleeting notion was the preamble to my inside bottom. My short phone conversation with Nicole in the car on the way to the hospital gave me the final nudge to that emotional inside rock bottom where I just could not live the way I was anymore. It was so scary in the moment, knowing that it was time to give up drinking. Soon after in the hospital I hit a point of resignation, where the courage to change was gifted to me. My fear dissolved. As I discussed in my story, I can't express to you the gravity of relief I felt in that moment. My whole dysfunctional relationship with drinking and using changed in that moment, so you never know what the catalyst will be for someone to hit their rock bottom and turn around for good.

WHAT DOES THIS HAVE TO DO WITH YOU?

You may witness your addict-alcoholic loved one hit many outside bottoms, continually doing things which damage themselves, their relationships, and their career, destroying their life. You can try to support them by suggesting they need help. You can even plan an intervention facilitated by a recovery center. All these things may help them take a step toward their own recovery, but at the end of the day, they must hit their own rock bottom to have their "awakening."

Keep speaking up to your addict-alcoholic loved one. They may get angry or defensive with you, and that is okay. It means you hit the mark. Every time you speak up, you chip away at their wall of delusion. One day, the cumulative effects of all the times you speak up may help their wall crumble. You may even help them get off the descending elevator of addiction a few floors sooner.

I know from my experience, every time my wife confronted me, I got angry and defensive. When she spoke up, it may not have worked in the moment, but over time the additive effects finally brought me to my knees and my rock-bottom moment where I awakened. It was my moment of surrender, which we will talk about next.

3.16 *COMPLIANCE* VERSUS *SURRENDER*

The type of bottom the addict-alcoholic hits (outside, inside, or rock bottom) plays a significant role in their attitude toward getting sober. The important question behind any action they take to get sober is this:

Are they doing it for themselves or to appease others?

Here is a quick story from a longtime friend of mine on this subject. Let's call him Robert.

* * *

Robert's story of his alcoholic mother:

"At my ultimatum, she finally agreed to go to rehab."

When I was in college, my parents divorced. Now that I was visiting my parents separately, they each had my full attention when I was with either of them. I started to notice my mom seemed to drink a lot. As I spent more time with her, I realized she was an alcoholic.

For the next thirty years of her drinking, she caused the usual types of problems of someone who drinks alcoholically. Sometimes she was drunk (in the middle of the day) when I brought my daughter to see her; I would get calls from the manager of the place she was staying at because she was drunk and acted up; and she tried to manipulate me and my sister all the time.

Fast forward to my middle-aged years, and whenever she called me or we had a visit, I was always on high alert. I was constantly looking for signs she had been drinking. Are her eyes glassy? Was that a stumble I just saw? Is she slurring? Unfortunately, most times the signs were there, and it was heartbreaking. I felt like I had lost my mother while she was still here on the planet.

My sisters and I tried so many times to broach the subject with our mother, and every time we did, the conversation seemed to go nowhere. She simply would not admit she needed help with her drinking. Then, one day after yet another drunk episode with Mom, I threatened to cut her off completely from seeing my daughter, her granddaughter. At my ultimatum, she finally agreed to go to rehab.

We did some research and found a place which could help her. When we called, they had a bed available. So, she packed up her things and I drove her in. After I dropped her off at rehab, I had mixed emotions driving home. I felt both victory and guilt at the same time. I literally said out loud "I WON!" while also feeling guilty for making my mom, the woman who gave birth to me and raised me, go to rehab.

Her rehab stint seemed to go well; we were told by the counselors that she did all the things they asked her to do. When Mom completed the program and was released, my sisters and I were looking forward to getting our mother back.

Pretty soon after getting out of rehab there were little red flags in her behavior, like not returning our calls for days or not remembering what we had talked about last time we chatted. It didn't seem like a big deal, so I chalked it up to her getting back on her feet. As it turns out, she started drinking again almost immediately after getting out of rehab and that's why she wasn't calling back or remembering what we talked about.

Reflecting from where I am today, I realize a few things kept me from seeing my mom's behavior for what it was after she got out of rehab:

- *First, my mom had become very good at controlling my perception of her. For decades she controlled the narrative of her drinking: denying it, lying about it, minimizing it, even guilting me at times. Though my gut instinct told me things weren't as she said, my logical mind would override my instinct and accept the lies and manipulation she was feeding me. Basically, I stopped trusting my instincts.*

- *Second, she was my mom ... the woman who gave birth to and raised me. The hope I had for her was born from love, and that hope clouded my ability to see the signs which were right in front of me.*

Unfortunately, at the time of writing this story she still has not found sobriety. I still have hope that will happen. I have been able to see her behavior for what it is: driven by the disease of addiction. I have stopped participating in her manipulative attempts and have set clear boundaries with her concerning her drinking. It breaks my heart to say this; I must keep a safe emotional distance from her to protect myself, my wife, and my daughter.

Today I still visit her (without my wife and daughter); however, our visits are kept short and are transactional. I have clearly let her know if she is drinking, I will not visit her. She has tested this boundary, and there have been times when I have turned around and left immediately because of her drinking. I accept my mother has a disease, and I am sad that the mother I knew when I was a child has been taken over by the disease of addiction. This all being said, I am in a good place and will still be a good son to her when she needs me, with the caveat that she is not drinking when I see her. I have "detached with love."

* * *

COMPLIANCE

Compliance for an addict-alcoholic means the push to get sober comes from a force outside of them. Their efforts to get sober are to appease others. It could be to hold onto their job, appease their partner who threatened to leave them, to satisfy an order from a judge, or in the case of the story above, to continue to see their grandchildren. At the end of the day whatever they do from a state of compliance, they do it begrudgingly. Compliance has a shelf life because there is still emotional resistance within them.

When getting sober out of compliance, deep down the addict-alcoholic still holds on to substances as their emotional coping mechanism. Because of that, most acting from a place of compliance end up using again.

An addict-alcoholic who is acting from a place of compliance has these typical thoughts and behaviors:

- They hold on to any of the misconceptions shown in the thought bubbles diagram in section 3.11 "Smashing the stereotype: the many flavors of addict-alcoholics."
- They *begrudgingly* go to recovery meetings, detox, or a 28-day rehab.
- They go to the minimum number of recovery meetings to keep people like you (or a judge) happy. For example, one meeting a week. How could a one-hour recovery meeting once a week help them with a problem they most likely indulged in every day for years or decades?

When in compliance, deep down the addict-alcoholic does not want to get sober and because of that most end up using again.

- When you ask them about the recovery meeting, they don't really engage in a conversation. They might give short answers like "I don't like those meetings" or "It was OK." The key is they don't really expand and share in detail what they heard.
- They look for reasons why the recovery meetings or programs are just "not for them." They may say things like "I am not like the people in those meetings" or "That works for other people, but I am different." This kind of thinking is common and in recovery meetings it's jokingly referred to as having "a case of terminal uniqueness." The recovery group's antidote to this type of thinking is the advice to "identify, don't compare."
- They do not take the suggestions given to them at the rehab or recovery meetings. They still try to compromise and do it "their way." My first sponsor in AA used to say to me, "Craig, your way didn't work out so well. Your way got you here; how about you try our way?"

After this negative discussion of compliance, I want to tell you something that I firmly believe:

Any reason for an addict-alcoholic to take actions toward recovery is a great reason. The hitch is that if they never transition from compliance to surrender, they will likely drink or use again.

The first step toward solid sobriety is physically breaking the cycle of drinking and using. Even when they begrudgingly try sobriety, the seed is planted. I have seen many people come into recovery to satisfy a court order (lightheartedly referred to in recovery programs as a "nudge from the judge"), then over time they hit an emotional surrender and got sober for good.

SURRENDER

When an addict-alcoholic hits an "outside bottom," they experience external consequences of their drinking and using. Outside bottoms are frequently not enough for them to make a change. "Inside bottoms" are a mental and emotional breakdown of sorts and can create one of the most important attitude shifts for an addict-alcoholic: *surrender*.

Surrender is an emotional state which an addict-alcoholic truly seeks recovery for themselves and nobody else. They start to let go of substances as their coping mechanism. It is when they become willing to do whatever it takes to develop new coping strategies. Surrender is an emotional requirement for them to truly seek recovery. They feel deep inside they just can't live the way they are anymore, and they become willing to do whatever it takes to change.

When an addict-alcoholic is in a state of surrender and seeking recovery, they are doing it because they want to. They are doing it for themselves and nobody else. In story after story, I hear people discuss how hitting their inside bottom triggered them to surrender and it was the catalyst for becoming a different person. When in a state of surrender, their chance of truly seeking recovery increases dramatically.

You may notice some of these characteristics when the addict-alcoholic in your life is acting from a place of surrender are:

- They freely admit they are an addict-alcoholic.

- They accept they cannot control their addiction, so they give up trying to control it and they try to abstain (they truly try "physical sobriety").
- They willingly go to detox or a 28-day rehab.
- They willingly go to multiple recovery meetings a week. They may even enjoy it.
- They consistently and sometimes enthusiastically share details of what they heard at the recovery meetings.
- Although the people in the meetings may be different from them (old/young, male/female, white collar/blue collar), they look for how they are the same. They may even say something like, "Those people understand me," or "I feel at home with those people because they are just like me."
- They actively work on developing new coping strategies by taking the suggestions given to them from the rehab or recovery meetings. This is where they start to attain "emotional sobriety."
- You notice them using new words and phrases they learned in the recovery meetings, things you have never heard them say before.
- You notice an emotional shift in them. You may not be able to put words to it; you may just feel they are different.

SURRENDER IS HARD BUT FREEING

The process of surrendering may be very scary for anybody, not just addict-alcoholics. Surrendering goes against everything our ego tells us to do.

We all want to think we have control over our lives, and the thought of surrender frequently invokes fear. The crazy thing about surrender is once you do it, fear dissolves and it's incredibly freeing.

In surrender you are no longer protecting anything. You don't feel the need to defend lies or hold up some image you are trying to portray. You are simply who you are, you take things as they come and you "go with the flow." I tell you from my experience, it takes a ton of effort to try to maintain the feeling of control. Once I surrendered, I had more energy. I didn't realize how exhausting it was to control everyone's perception of me, especially my wife Nicole's perception. I have found surrender so much more relaxing because I let things unfold as they will without trying to control them.

WHAT DOES THIS HAVE TO DO WITH YOU?

The answer to this question is hope. Your hope. Your love, concern, and heartbreak for them is so strong you want to see some progress toward sobriety, *any progress.* It is natural for your hope to overinflate any tiny effort the addict-alcoholic makes in the direction of recovery. Even when they are forced into a detox or rehab by outside circumstances (the police, a judge, an overdose, or health problems from using), your hope that this time "it will stick" strengthens.

I am not saying you shouldn't hope, and I don't think it's possible for us humans not to have hope when we see something positive. I am saying to protect yourself from further heartbreak and disappointment, temper your expectations, which starts with answering the following question honestly:

Is their effort toward recovery coming from a place of compliance or a state of surrender?

To protect yourself, temper your expectations. Start with answering the compliance versus surrender question honestly.

For people like you, hope can interfere with your ability to answer the compliance versus surrender question honestly. Namely, you grab onto any small reason to tell yourself, "This time they will get sober for good." Hope can blind you from seeing the situation for what it is. Obvious red flags escape your perception. Because of hope blindness, when you try to help them, you may be unintentionally enabling them. Then if they relapse you just don't understand where things went wrong, and you end up feeling angry, crushed, or betrayed once again.

Here is a story about my parents and my oldest brother Glenn.

* * *

My parents' hope enabled my brother Glenn:

"Despite all his knowledge on addiction, my dad was still blinded by hope when it came to his own son."

My oldest brother Glenn struggled mightily with addiction. Toward the end of his active using days, his partner Eileen kicked him out and he was living with my parents—for free. Every time I talked to my parents on the phone, they would glow about any little effort my brother made toward sobriety. There were family events where my brother was obviously intoxicated, and both my parents just couldn't see it.

Hope for their son had blinded my parents to what was unfolding right in front of our eyes. My dad had been in recovery for over twenty-eight years at that point, so he knew how to spot an addict-alcoholic. He was an example of just how strong hope can be. Despite all his knowledge on addiction, my dad was still blinded by hope when it came to his own son.

Sometimes when I would call home, my mom's hopes would be soaring. With much enthusiasm, she would say things like: "Your brother Glenn went to an AA meeting this week!" I remember thinking: Great, he is still messed up every time I see him. He is drinking and using right under your noses, and you are helping him do it by giving him a free ride.

My parents' enabling of my brother continued for a while by not seeing the signs of his using and allowing him to live with them for free. Eventually my brother sank so deep my parents had no choice but to finally see the situation for what it was, and their blinding hope was smashed. They kicked him out. My mother took Glenn's drinking and using personally; she thought the support they were giving him should have been enough. She was very resentful. She didn't know his using wasn't personal, and that my brother had to hit his own rock bottom to surrender.

My brother eventually did hit his own rock bottom, surrendered, and has been sober for over 5 years now.

* * *

The question of compliance versus surrender is not black and white. If you go back through the two lists of characteristics for compliance and surrender, you may find the addict-alcoholic in your life has characteristics from both. This is usually the case.

So, how do you figure out where they are when it comes to compliance versus surrender? This is why it's important for you to have a support network. Someone outside of your situation, and who has been through a similar experience, can help you see things clearly. This is where Al-Anon (or Nar-Anon for drug addicts) helps tremendously.

3.17 HOW CAN YOU HELP THE ADDICT-ALCOHOLIC?

Your desire to help your addicted loved one could be a big reason you are reading *Beyond the Lies.* I will help you with this. In order to properly answer the question, we need to understand more about the dynamics of your relationship with the addict-alcoholic.

In short, the addict-alcoholic has pushed your relationship to an unhealthy state. Trust and honesty are most likely gone. You feel the lack of trust, and perhaps you have a gut feeling they are not being honest with you.

Until you learn what has made your relationship unhealthy and gain some tools to make it healthy again, it will be difficult for you to help them. I have heard a metaphor for this:

There is a person trapped at the bottom of a well. They are yelling with the hope someone will hear them. A passerby hears the calls and comes to help. The passerby has two options:

1. Go down into the well and try to help them out, or,

2. Find a rope to pull the stuck person out.

If the passerby goes into the well to help, now there are two people stuck in the well. When the passerby knows about being stuck in a well, they know not to go down in themselves. They know to use a rope instead. When they use a rope there is one person stuck in the well and one person legitimately helping.

In the metaphor, the well represents your unhealthy relationship with the addict-alcoholic. When you knowingly or unknowingly engage in the unhealthy relationship, you are going down into the well with them. When you stay out of unhealthy behaviors, you are not joining them in the well. This enables you to use a rope and truly help.

So, let's talk more about how your relationship with them, and yourself has become unhealthy.

CHAPTER 4:

Enough About Them, What About You?! (Your Role)

4.1 THE "IDENTIFIED PATIENT"

I have gone to many therapists in my life seeking help, especially when I was actively drinking and using. I wanted something else, anything, besides alcohol and drugs to be the problem because I didn't want to quit them. One thing I learned in therapy is the concept of the "identified patient."

The identified patient is the person in the family system who has the obvious problem. They are the person who everyone else can point their finger to and say, "Look at how mentally ill they are" or "They are the cause of all our problems."

What ends up happening is the finger pointers are so busy blaming the identified patient for their problems that they never take a good look at themselves.

The addict-alcoholic is the obvious identified patient in any family system. Frequently the focus of the loved ones is 100% on the addict-alcoholic. Your thoughts and what you talk to other people about become dominated by the current status of the addict-alcoholic.

Can you relate to any of the questions or statements below?

- Is he drunk or high again?
- Is she OK to drive?
- They were supposed to be home by now; I hope they didn't get in trouble. I want to call them to make sure they are OK.
- Is he going to be a happy drunk or an angry drunk this time?
- I hope she doesn't get herself fired from work.
- Do I have to drive his butt home *again* because he got so drunk or high?
- Should I invite her to my party? I'm afraid she's going to get too intoxicated and make a scene.

When you talk to other people, are the conversations frequently dominated by the topic of the addict-alcoholic and what state they are in?

It is common for people like you to become so obsessed with watching and analyzing their behavior that you lose touch with yourself. The loved

While the addict or alcoholic is obsessed with alcohol or drugs, the loved ones become obsessed with the addict-alcoholic's behavior.

ones get so lost in the situation, you lose the ability to listen to what your senses and intuition are telling you; you can't accept what is right in front of you. You may even blame them for *all* your problems.

Your obsession with the addict-alcoholic's behavior becomes your addiction and it has made you sick too. You have gone (and are going) through a traumatic experience, and you can benefit from healing.

4.2 SUPPORT FROM THE FAMILY GROUPS OF AL-ANON AND NAR-ANON

Al-Anon is a support group for the loved ones of alcoholics and was started in 1951 by the family members of the people who started Alcoholics Anonymous. Nar-Anon was started in 1968 to support family members of drug users. Members of Al-Anon and Nar-Anon are from all walks of life.

They are wives, husbands, siblings, parents, and friends of addict-alcoholics. They are lawyers, laborers, caretakers, doctors, store owners, plumbers, and accountants.

They facilitate meetings where the family members of addict-alcoholics connect and provide support for each other. The more experienced members help the newer members navigate the messy landscape of living with an addict-alcoholic. Al-Anon helped my wife tremendously.

The biggest mistake newcomers to Al-Anon or Nar-Anon make is they don't give the group a fair chance. The family member might go to just a few meetings and decide it is not for them. If you really give the group an honest effort, you will absolutely find somebody who has been through what you have. You will meet someone who understands you, has felt exactly the way you do, and can help you feel better.

Al-Anon and Nar-Anon members are people just like you, who are worried about someone with a drinking or drug problem.

One of the most important first steps to receiving benefit from these groups is described in a saying you will hear there: "Identify and don't compare." It means to look for where you are the same as the other members. When you look to identify, you brush aside your differences such as gender, socio-economic background, and relation to the addict-alcoholic (partner/spouse versus sibling versus parent, etc.). You open yourself up to benefit from what they have to offer you.

When you compare yourself to the other members, you look for differences as to why your situation is unique. When comparing you look for reasons why "they just don't understand you." The differences become the focal point of your thought process and the door to receiving any benefit is slammed shut.

Both groups are all over the world; their websites are below. They have a quiz there to help you understand how you have been affected and how they can help.

https://al-anon.org/

https://www.nar-anon.org/

4.3 THEIR ADDICTION IS NOT YOUR FAULT

The statement the title is making can be controversial, as trauma and addiction frequently go hand in hand. Many addict-alcoholics have turned to substances to cope with trauma. If you have caused trauma to your addicted loved one, it would be beneficial and freeing to heal the wounds from whatever happened together with your loved one, whether through therapy or other recovery means.

> This discussion in this section applies more to the loved ones who have not caused trauma to the addict-alcoholic.

When it comes to the addict-alcoholic's drinking and using because of trauma, they are ultimately responsible for that. Yes, they may be using to cope with trauma; however, there are much healthier ways to deal with trauma and it's their decision which path they take.

The discussion in this section applies more to the loved ones who have not caused trauma to the addict-alcoholic.

In the cases where you have not caused trauma to the addict-alcoholic, you may still have a deep feeling of responsibility for their situation. Contrary to what you might feel, the addict-alcoholic in your life does not use or drink because of you.

There is nothing you did or didn't do to cause your loved one's addiction.

Even as I tell you this, you may still have feelings of embarrassment, shame, or guilt, thinking you "could have done more." Their addiction wasn't caused by anyone else. It was not caused by something bad which happened to them. Addict-alcoholics use the way they do for one reason only: they have the disease of addiction because chemicals are their only tool for coping.

I am not saying that any trauma they may have experienced doesn't push them toward alcohol or drugs for relief. Section 3.6 "Why do addict-alcoholics use?" broke down the disease of addiction. What didn't you see there as a reason? You! That's because none of it is your fault.

Now, the addict-alcoholic in your life may have tried to make you feel like you were the cause. Even if they have not directly blamed you, your own brain may do it for them. Whether it's them blaming you, or you blaming yourself, here are common themes I hear when talking to loved ones who accept responsibility for their loved ones using:

- I didn't love them enough.
- I didn't show up to their games enough.
- I did not spend enough time with them.
- I was a nag.
- I should have been a better partner.

Can you identify with any of those thoughts?

My dad used to repeat a quote he heard in recovery which fits well here: "Don't believe everything you think."

Just remember, their using is not because of you, anybody else, any situation, or anything else. They have the disease of addiction because they have not dealt with their life trauma and emotional baggage in a healthier way.

4.4 YOU CAN'T CONTROL THEIR ADDICTION

It is heartbreaking for people like you to be around an addicted loved one who repeatedly makes their situation worse. At the same time, you may be angry with them for all the turmoil they have caused you and the household. It's not fair to the family. You have heavy, sometimes conflicting emotions floating around inside of you because of their behavior. It is natural for you to want to be rid of those emotions.

A common first step by people like you to manage the situation is to try to help them control their disease. Have you ever tried to help your addicted loved one by doing anything like the following?

- Monitored their drinking or using and told them when it's time to stop.
- Dumped their alcohol down the drain.
- Threw out their stash.
- Did anything to shield or protect them from drinking or using.

Unfortunately, none of those things ever work. Despite your best intentions, your attempts to control their using will only foster resentment from the addict-alcoholic. They may say nasty things to you if you do any of the things listed above. I know because I went through this with my partner when I was actively using!

Multiple sections in chapter 3 discussed how addict-alcoholics are powerless over their disease. They take one drink, the craving kicks in, and the craving drives them to drink more.

If they can't control their disease, how could you control it for them?

Until the addict-alcoholic hits their inside bottom (as discussed in section 3.15 "What is hitting rock bottom?") they will always find a way to get more of what they need and use it.

Your peace and serenity depend on your ability to accept the things you cannot change.

Your unsuccessful attempts at controlling their using may foster feelings of powerlessness in you. You may not realize how much energy you are exerting to control something which is out of your control. As your attempts fail, more feelings of powerlessness may drive you to try even harder in your efforts. Many people like you end up becoming obsessed with the addict-alcoholic's using. Exerting all that mental energy is exhausting.

This is how loved ones like you become sick too. You are so focused on them, you don't take care of yourself. You lose touch with yourself. Signs you are trying to control their disease and not taking care of yourself are:

- constant irritability, anger, or quick temper
- difficulty sleeping
- tired all the time

- feelings of hopelessness or desperation

You simply can't control their addiction. So, what can you control?

You have control over your own actions and responses. Or, sometimes more importantly, you have control over your own inactions and lack of responses! Sometimes not rescuing them or saying anything to them is the best path forward for you.

Your first job is to allow the addict-alcoholic their journey. This doesn't mean you like it or approve of what they are doing. We have discussed what it means for an addict-alcoholic to hit bottom, which can be a critical turning point in their life. One of my trusted advisors in recovery has a saying:

"I would hate to deny somebody their bottom."

If you give the addict-alcoholic the space to hit their own bottom, it is highly possible your own feelings of powerlessness will scream at you. You feel compelled to "help." But what is the real reason you want to help them? A common trap people like you fall into is that frequently "helping" is confused with simply trying to exert some control to make yourself feel better. Because your loved one's disease is out of control, you try to "help" to quell your own feelings of powerlessness.

Resist your urges to exert some form of control over the situation. I know it is very difficult for you to stand by and watch your loved one sink into addict-alcoholic despair without trying to help. Remember, allowing them to hit their bottom can be the best thing that ever happens to them. As I look back, I can honestly say the complete and utter despair I felt when I hit my bottom was the biggest turning point my life has ever seen.

The key message in this section is simple:

Trying to control the addict-alcoholic's using does not work and will only cause you more angst.

4.5 IT IS NOT YOUR JOB TO FIX THE ADDICT-ALCOHOLIC

Can you relate to any of the questions below?

- Have you ever tried to help the addict-alcoholic in your life, and their reaction was seemingly unappreciative?
- Did they ever become irritable or angry when you tried to help?
- Or, after all the effort you put in to get them into a detox or rehab, did you feel frustration or resentment when they drank or used again after they got out?

Let's share more about Robert's story with his mother from section 3.16 "Compliance versus surrender."

* * *

Robert's big realization:

"I surrendered to the fact that no matter what I did, my mom was going to do what she wanted to do."

When my sisters and I got my mom into rehab, we really felt like we won the battle with her drinking. As part of the rehab program, they facilitated counseling sessions with the whole family present. In our first meeting with the counselor, he spe-

cifically stated that Mom had a disease, and it was possible she would drink again. The feeling that we had "won" quickly dissolved. One of my sisters did not want to accept that and started making demands of Mom. The case worker instantly stopped my sister. He said demands and ultimatums by the family will never work. I had a nagging thought that a big reason my mom was in rehab was because of the ultimatum I made about not seeing her granddaughter again.

He urged us to be supportive of my mom, even while we were all anxious that she could very well start drinking again. It was during this conversation with the counselor that I learned no matter what my sisters and I do, we have no control over what my mom actually does. It was an enlightening thought, a moment of awakening for me.

I knew the tough part for us would be how to love and support her if she started drinking again. Unfortunately, I had to cross that bridge shortly after Mom got out of rehab. As a matter of fact, as I mentioned earlier, she has never really stopped drinking on her own. She has had stints of abstaining from alcohol, but those were usually because she was either in rehab or in trouble with the law when she got caught drunk driving.

Looking back on it, I have certainly had thoughts that maybe if I did things differently, my mom would be sober. I have since learned there is no right or wrong with these things and accepted that I did the best I could at the time.

The other realization I had is that Mom never bought into admitting she had a disease and that it was up to her to work on the things she was trying to numb with alcohol. Her mental and emotional issues—anxiety and depression—were never really properly treated beyond medication. My mom for some reason never wanted to do therapy. It was a deep stigma for her. She was embarrassed (she said this quite often) and wanted to hide this part of her life from friends and family.

I always felt like we kids were doing all the work to get her better, not my mom. That was the kicker, right? And we were really upset about that. But over time, I took the case worker's advice when he told us that making my mom better was not my job. I started focusing on my own mental health and what made me happy. I surrendered to the fact that no matter what I did, my mom was going to do what she wanted to do. It was a pivotal moment in my life. I was still both angry and sad about what she was doing to herself, but I made sure I focused on the positive things in my life: my family, friends, and making music.

* * *

I see family members try to fix the addict-alcoholic in their life all the time. This can be shown by the following forms of behavior:

- trying to control their using (as we discussed in the previous section),
- working harder than they do to find them professional help like a detox, rehab, or sober house, or
- managing their recovery efforts in general (such as constantly pushing them to go to recovery meetings).

If they don't want to be helped, the more you try to help them, the more they may act out toward you or pull away from you. Unfortunately, you can't fix them, especially when they don't want help. When it comes to your role in helping them, here is the crux of this discussion:

Fixing the addict-alcoholic is not your job.

They must hit their bottom to seek recovery, and nobody can do that for them.

If your effort exceeds theirs, it's a huge red flag they don't want it. Just take note of how much effort you are putting forth versus how much effort they are. When your effort outweighs theirs, the probability of success for what you are doing to help them is very low. It may even foster resentment from them. The saying from Al-Anon "detach with love" applies here.

For those of you who have addict-alcoholic children, this is against your parental instincts. I am not saying you shouldn't support your addicted child to get sober and seek recovery. As a loving mother or father, you are in a position to be very helpful!

As your expectations go up, your peace and serenity will go down.

When you do help, be mindful to let go of any expectations. What they do with your help is not up to you. Expectations that your efforts will fix the addict-alcoholic set you up for disappointment. If they reluctantly accept your help and there seems to be progress toward sobriety, you feel hope building inside you. Then, when they show up drunk or high again you end up with feelings of resentment and helplessness.

You have taken on responsibility for their sobriety, and it doesn't work. This is a common scenario for the loved ones of addict-alcoholics. You only have power over your own reactions to their behavior and to take care of yourself.

Al-Anon has a saying which summarizes the discussions from the last three sections:

> ***"You didn't cause it, you can't control it,***
> ***and you can't cure it."***

4.6 WHAT DOES "ENABLING ADDICT-ALCOHOLICS" MEAN?

Many loved ones of addict-alcoholics don't realize some of the things they do to "help" is really enabling. It is not surprising because frequently there is a fine line between supporting and enabling. The Merriam-Webster dictionary defines an "enabler" as:

> <u>**Enabler**</u>:
>
> 1. One that enables another to achieve an end, *especially*: one who enables another to persist in self-destructive behavior (such as substance abuse) by providing excuses or by **making it possible to avoid the consequences of such behavior**.[3]

The last part of the definition is the key. Any action on your part which helps the addict-alcoholic avoid the consequences of using is enabling. The tricky part for you is what may seem like helping could indirectly be enabling. An example of this is buying food for an addict because they don't have any money. The truth is they don't have money because they spent it

---

3 "enabler." *Merriam-Webster.com,* 2025. https://www.merriam-webster.com.

on drugs or alcohol. By providing food, you enable them to keep buying drugs with whatever money they have.

I came across an article on VeryWellMind.com which helps further define enabling. In the article written by Buddy T, who has decades of experience, he states:

> "Helping is doing something for someone that they are not capable of doing themselves. Enabling is doing for someone things that they could and should be doing themselves."[4]

I like how Buddy describes it. Based on his definition, what constitutes helping versus enabling varies depending on the specific situation and your relationship with the addict-alcoholic. Let's talk about some of the different forms of enabling I have run across; some of the forms go far beyond what you may think.

1) Helping the addict-alcoholic procure drugs or alcohol.

Whether you buy a large bottle of hard liquor or just their favorite six-pack of beer, getting any amount of drugs or alcohol for them is directly enabling their using. If you drive them to get drugs or alcohol because they can't drive themselves (too intoxicated or lost license due to an OUI), this is also direct enabling.

---

4 Buddy T., "How to Recognize Enabling," *VeryWellMind.com*, accessed June 20, 2025, https://www.verywellmind.com/enabling-alcoholic-is-not-helping-63297.

Lending them money is a form of indirect enabling. Many addict-alcoholics have money problems from spending it on substances and not having a stable income because they can't hold jobs. They might tell you the money is for rent, food, or some other bill associated with normal living. The reality is, most of the time when they ask for money it is to buy drugs or alcohol. Even when the request for money is really to pay their bills, if you lend them money (or pay the bills for them), you are enabling them to spend whatever money they have on substances.

Anything which directly or indirectly helps them procure drugs and alcohol is enabling.

2) Assuming the role of permanent designated driver.

When you go out with the addict-alcoholic in your life, you may notice that you get into the driver's seat without even thinking about it. You may not want the role of designated driver, and yet you do it. Perhaps you have an unconscious knowledge that allowing them to drive is not safe. If you seem to always be the designated driver, you are sending a message to the addict-alcoholic they have a green light to use.

3) Fixing any problems the addict-alcoholic caused because of their addiction (rescuing).

Have you ever done anything like the following?

- Gone out of your way to drive the addict-alcoholic around because they lost their license.
- Lent them your car because they damaged theirs from driving while intoxicated.

- Helped with police troubles or legal troubles.
- Tried to fix their problems at work.
- Smoothed things over with other people for them.

Addict-alcoholics often create a lengthy list of problems for themselves. When you try to fix those problems for them, you are enabling. Any time you shield them from the natural consequences of their behavior, you are enabling. Most loved ones of addict-alcoholics feel compelled to rescue them by fixing the problems, so if you have done it, you are not alone. *Fixing their problems is not your job. When you do that, it's enabling!*

Seeing a loved one suffer is difficult. Our natural response is to try to "help" them. When it comes to active addiction, rescuing them teaches the addict-alcoholic the consequences of their using will be minimized *for* them. So, in their mind it is OK to keep using; someone will take care of them.

Additionally, your well-intentioned caretaking could prevent the very consequence which helps them hit bottom and start their journey to recovery. My recovery sponsor has a saying:

"I would hate to prevent anybody from hitting their bottom."

When you allow them to feel the consequences of their behavior and don't bail them out, you may get some backlash. This is especially true if you have a history of rescuing them. When you stop enabling them in this way, they might get frustrated or angry. They might yell at you or try emotionally manipulating you. Have you ever heard them say, "How could you leave me in a time like this?" or "All I am asking you to do is help me"?

Remember, the addict-alcoholic's problems are not yours to fix.

4) Covering for them by making excuses to others (another type of rescuing).

Have you ever done anything like the following?

- Lied to other people because you were embarrassed for the addict-alcoholic in your life.
- Stood up for your child when they got in trouble because of drugs or alcohol, saying they are just a kid and kids make mistakes.
- Called into your partner's work for them when they were hungover to give excuses on why they weren't going in that day.

If you have done anything similar to what I list above, you are not alone! It's a common occurrence I see with the family members. Shame, which was discussed in section 3.4: "The shame with the words *addict* and *alcoholic*," can drive people like you to make excuses for the addict-alcoholic. Despite the progress over the past few decades at de-shaming addiction, shame and embarrassment are still alive and well when it comes to the disease of addiction.

Another reason you might make excuses for the addict-alcoholic is that they can discreetly and easily manipulate you into doing it. A child might plead innocent ignorance. A partner might casually say, "Honey, do you mind calling into my work for me? I feel terrible and can't deal with that right now." Even with the best intentions in mind, when you make excuses for them which prevent or alleviate emotional pain, you are enabling.

A great example of covering for the addict-alcoholic by making excuses for them is my story in section 3.4 "The shame with the words addict or alcoholic." My mother lied to all my relatives (and us kids) when my oldest brother was not at my cousin's wedding to prevent my brother from feeling emotional pain and herself from facing shame.

Don't feel bad if you have shame; we all have it to some extent! The key is to be aware of it and not let it drive your behavior because it can push you toward actions which enable the addict-alcoholic.

Another reason you might make excuses for the addict-alcoholic is the discomfort which comes with seeing loved ones feel emotional pain. It's part of the human condition. It is hard to allow them to suffer the consequences of their using. A natural tendency is to try to alleviate or prevent the emotional pain from happening. This is especially true for the parents of addict-alcoholic children.

Remember their emotional pain is needed to push them toward hitting their bottom, which can spark their big turnaround. Preventing the addict-alcoholic from hitting their bottom takes away their motivation to get sober.

5) Managing the addict-alcoholic's life for them (another form of rescuing).

Can you relate to anything like the following?

- Have you ever repeatedly reminded the addict-alcoholic about appointments or things they agreed to do because you don't trust they will do them?

- Have you taken over the important household chores like paying bills or picking up the kids because you don't trust them to perform the duty?

Managing the addict-alcoholic's life for them sends the message that even if they are incapacitated from using, there are no consequences. When you do this, the message you send is it's OK for them to keep using the way they are.

6) Allowing yourself to be manipulated.

You might bristle at my above statement; I ask you to please just reflect on it without your ego involved. Your mental and emotional health depends on it! Can you relate to any of the questions below?

- Have you ever kept quiet when you felt the addict-alcoholic has lied to you or one of their excuses just didn't seem right?
- When you tried to hold them accountable for their behavior, have they ever guilt tripped you and it worked?
- Have you ever called them out on their using and they changed the subject on you?
- Have you ever smelled drugs or alcohol on them when you didn't see them use and you didn't say anything?
- Have you ever confronted the addict-alcoholic about their using, their response was to point out your flaws, and then you defended yourself?

If you had experiences like any of those questions above, it's a subtle clue you have participated in their manipulation. Don't judge yourself if you have; addict-alcoholics are masters at coaxing their loved ones into their manipulation schemes.

Remember it takes two people for manipulation to happen: one to manipulate and one to be manipulated. You may not realize the depth of manipulation you might have been subjected to.

7) Downplaying the addict-alcoholic's substance abuse problem to yourself (self-delusion).

When you minimize in your own mind what is happening with the addict-alcoholic, you are deluding yourself into thinking the situation is not as bad as it really is. Remember the discussions we had about delusion; it means you believe yourself even though what you are convincing yourself of is not true. You unconsciously do it to alleviate your own emotions and to protect the addict-alcoholic.

Sometimes people like you can't accept the extent of the addict-alcoholic's substance abuse problem because it is emotionally overwhelming. You want to believe they are better than they really are, and this blinds you. You just don't see and register their obvious signs of addiction. The story of my brother Glenn living with my parents in section 3.16 demonstrated this. They were completely blinded by hope and did not notice his red eyes or the weird gait he walked with when he was messed up. You rationalize their addiction-driven behaviors as caused by anything but addiction.

The addict-alcoholic will sense you don't want to believe what's going on, so to protect their ability to keep using they will absolutely manipulate you further to reinforce your self-delusion.

My brother Glenn sensed this with my parents so one thing he would do was the opposite of downplaying his substance use. He would "up-play" any tiny effort he put toward recovery. Whenever he went to an AA meeting (which wasn't often), he would make a big deal about it. By capitalizing on my parents' hope, he successfully shifted their attention away from his red eyes or slightly slurred speech and onto what he was "doing" to get better (even though what he was doing was just a show).

Let's hear another story. Maria is a friend of mine, and she is the mother of a son who was a teenage addict. Maria shares her experience and walks you through how it affected her. I ask you to identify with Maria and don't compare. Try to see where you have had similar experiences or felt the same way she did.

* * *

Maria's story of self-delusion:

"He said he just wanted to go for a drive and listen to music to clear his mind."

My son struggled with drugs starting around the age of 14. After a few years and multiple incidents with the police, he was court ordered to go to rehab. The day my son was coming home from rehab, there was noticeable tension in the house. We were all nervous about what he would be like. My husband and I went to pick him up. As he came out, I could immediately sense he was back to his old self. He had that sparkle in his eye that he used to have. I felt a tremendous sense of relief.

The first few weeks went great. I was elated; I seemed to finally have my son back. The tension in the whole house had dissolved. Then he started getting quiet and reclusive again. He would still go to recovery meetings, so I told myself he just needed time to readjust to life without drugs.

One night, he asked to use the car, so naturally I asked him, "What for?" He said he just wanted to go for a drive and listen to music to clear his mind. It was around 4 or 5 p.m. so we didn't think anything of it and said yes.

By 7 p.m. he had not returned home yet. That nagging feeling in my stomach started again, telling me that things were not right. By 9 p.m. he still hadn't returned home; then we received a call from him. He went through a stop sign and broadsided a truck in an industrial park. The car was totaled from the accident, so my husband and I went to pick him up.

On the way there, I had the gut feeling that to "clear one's mind," a country drive or a drive to the beach seemed more appropriate than a deserted industrial park at 9 p.m. I didn't want to believe what my intuition was telling me.

When my son got in our car, he was sobbing, thinking he could have killed the other driver. He kept repeating that he was just out for a drive to clear his head, listening to music when it happened.

My uneasy feelings continued, and my instincts were screaming that he was using again. But my broken heart overrode that, and I convinced myself to believe that he was out for an innocent drive. I ended up calling a friend of mine in recovery and relayed what happened. My friend told me what he thought the truth was: my son was using again and was in that industrial park to get drugs. I was angry at what he said, even though I already knew he was right. So, I directed my anger toward my friend in recovery and didn't talk to him for a while.

A week later, my son had very bad stomach pain because he was having trouble going to the bathroom, so I took him to the hospital. When the doctor came in, my son asked me to step out while he talked to the doctor. When I was asked to come back in, my son confirmed what I already knew but didn't want to believe. He said, "I am going through withdrawals, and I need help." We took him to rehab that day.

As his mother, I always want the best for my son. Reflecting back, I now see how my unconditional love and hope for my son caused me to delude myself and believe what he was telling me even though I knew I shouldn't believe him. Today I know I was enabling him by believing his excuses. But let me tell you, as his mother, it was SO HARD in the moment to stand in my truth and say what my instincts and logical mind were telling me.

* * *

Maria's story shows how the loved ones may develop very strong self-delusions. Even when others directly tell people like you the truth, your delusion rejects what you are hearing. This is why support from other people who have been in your situation can really help you break out of your self-delusion. In section 4.2 we talked about the family support groups of Al-Anon and Nar-Anon. Both groups have meetings which is a great place to find people who have been through what you are going through.

REFLECTIONS FOR THE TOPIC OF ENABLING

Review the checklist below and check off anything which reminds you of something you have done. It may not be the exact thing in the list, but check it off if you have experienced anything familiar. If you are able to check more than 1 or 2 boxes, please consider how your behavior has enabled the addict-alcoholic.

- ☐ Have you ever bought alcohol or drugs for the addict-alcoholic?
- ☐ Have you ever lent them money?
- ☐ Are you routinely the designated driver?
- ☐ Have you ever made excuses to other people for the addict-alcoholic's drunk or high behavior at a party (or some other function)?
- ☐ Have you ever driven them because they lost their license?
- ☐ Have you consistently reminded them of their appointments or duties to make sure they got them done?
- ☐ Have you ever taken care of their duties for them because it just seemed easier to do it yourself?
- ☐ Have you taken over making sure the bills are paid on time?
- ☐ When the addict-alcoholic has had problems with the police or any other people, have you ever stepped in to try to smooth things over? Have you ever bailed them out of jail?
- ☐ Have you ever kept quiet when you thought the addict-alcoholic was lying to you or something just didn't seem right?

4.7 WHAT IS "GASLIGHTING"?

Gaslighting is a type of manipulation. If you have an addict-alcoholic in your life, you have most likely been gaslighted, so let's define it.

The Merriam-Webster dictionary defines gaslighting as:

Gaslighting:

1. Psychological manipulation of a person usually over an extended period of time that causes the victim to question the validity of their own thoughts, perception of reality, or memories and typically leads to confusion, loss of confidence and self-esteem…."[5]

Gaslighting is a subtle form of psychological and emotional abuse with devastating effects.

To gaslight you, the addict-alcoholic does not have to definitively prove your perception is wrong, they just need to plant seeds of doubt in your mind.

When you are being gaslighted, your intuition might be telling you there is something not quite right about the situation, but self-doubt makes you question your own perception and gut instincts. Once you are in a state of self-doubt, it opens the door for the addict-alcoholic to manipulate you.

Here's a simple example of addict-alcoholic gaslighting:

---

5 "gaslighting." *Merriam-Webster.com*, 2025, www.merriam-webster.com.

You: *"You really got drunk at the party last night. I don't like it when you do that."*

Addict-alcoholic: *"Oh c'mon, I wasn't that bad. Plus, I didn't sleep well the night before, so I was exhausted."*

The short statement by the addict-alcoholic is packed with manipulation, so let's take a closer look at it.

- You first stated what your eyes and ears told you about what happened at the party: *"You got really drunk at the party last night."*
- You followed it up with how you feel about it: *"I don't like it when you do that."*
- The first part of the addict-alcoholic's response was to **imply** you were overreacting when he said, *"Oh c'mon."* The implication is you think it was worse than it really was, and your perception is off (gaslighting).
- Then, they **directly** said your perception was not correct (gaslighting again) when they followed with, *"I wasn't that bad."*
- Next, they created what seems like a feasible alternative scenario as to why you may have seen what you saw with the excuse of: *"Plus, I didn't sleep well the night before, so I was exhausted."* Even if they completely made up the feasible alternative scenario, there are now two potential "realities" of what happened last night.
- Since you may not have proof they are lying about the lack of sleep, you can't disprove the alternative scenario. This is the cracked door through which your self-doubt

creeps in. You start to question what your own eyes and ears told you at the party.

So, maybe you read the example above and think you wouldn't fall for that. I agree with you if it's once or twice. But what if the addict-alcoholic constantly did things like this for months or years?

Gaslighting causes a slow erosion of your sense of self.

Over an extended period of time, gaslighting works and it makes you question your senses, values, intuition, and guiding principles. Essentially, you lose your personal map for navigating tough situations with your addicted loved one, and now they can control you.

Addict-alcoholics have many ways to gaslight you. The next few chapters will introduce you to addict-alcoholic manipulation.

CHAPTER 5:

Addict-Alcoholics Are Expert Manipulators

5.1 WHY DO ADDICT-ALCOHOLICS MANIPULATE?

If you are the loved one of an addict-alcoholic, please know that twenty-four hours a day, seven days a week, they think and plan (consciously and unconsciously) when, where, and how they can use. What this means for you is that if you are trying to outsmart them, you are playing checkers while they are playing chess. I know this because I did this to my wife. Drinking and using was constantly on my mind when I was "active." She didn't have a chance when it came to confronting me.

If anybody gets in the way of using or drinking, the addict-alcoholic needs to find some way to get around the block. What constitutes a "block"? It could be that you question them on their using or something as seemingly innocuous as wanting to spend time with them. If they need to go see their drug dealer, or they need to drink during the day, how can they do that if you are with them? The solution to their dilemma? Manipulation.

Their manipulation stems from the fear of not being able to drink or drug the way they *need to.* The fear is rooted in physical addiction (biology) and emotional reliance (psychology) on chemicals to cope with life. If they don't get what they need, they will start feeling physical detox symptoms. If they don't get what they need, they will start feeling emotions.

In doing research, I came across a perfect description of how manipulation is executed, especially by addict-alcoholics. It is on vocabulary.com:

Manipulation:

"Exerting shrewd or devious influence especially for one's own advantage…**a manipulative person knows how to twist words, play on emotions and otherwise manage a situation in a sneaky fashion to get what he wants.**"[6]

The first story I shared about myself in chapter one described to you what was going on inside me when I was manipulating Nicole during my active drinking and using years.

When the addict-alcoholic manipulates, they may not be consciously thinking, *I am going to manipulate this person now.* Their fear of not being able to use activates their "fight-or-flight" survival response, and they will do whatever it

6 "manipulation." *Vocabulary.com,* 2025. https://www.vocabulary.com.

takes to drink or use. Manipulation becomes as automatic as breathing; they do it without thinking about it. I have heard this quote many times in recovery meetings:

"I lied so often that it became part of me.
I lied even when I didn't have to."

The top reasons why addict-alcoholics manipulate are:

1. to protect their ability to use the way they need to, and

2. because manipulation works.

Almost all human beings manipulate to some degree. The difference for addict-alcoholics is manipulation becomes a tool which they hone and master. At times the scheme is premeditated, multifaceted, and elaborate. Other times it is reactionary and occurs "on the fly." Some manipulation tactics are outrageous and "in your face," while other times they are sneaky and below the surface.

This is a fact:

If you are the loved one of an addict-alcoholic,
you have been chronically subjected to manipulation.

5.2 WHY LEARN ABOUT HOW ADDICT-ALCOHOLICS MANIPULATE?

Can you relate to any of these questions?

- When it comes to the addict-alcoholic in your life have you ever had feelings of suspicion, confusion, or anger?
- When you are around the addict-alcoholic, do you find it hard to relax or that you are on high alert?

- Do you have this nagging feeling that things are not what they seem with your addicted loved one, but you don't say anything?
- Or did you say something and they scared you off with anger, or came up with some plausible explanation that still didn't feel right to you but you let it go?
- Do you have any of the physical symptoms of chronic manipulation like difficulty sleeping, inability to relax, constant irritability, or you feel exhausted all the time?

Remember how I started this chapter: addict-alcoholics are driven to think about using twenty-four hours a day, seven days a week. How can the family and friends compete with that? The answer is that you can't no matter how hard you try, and trying will only make you sick too. This is one of the reasons why addiction is often referred to as a family disease. The end result is that the addict-alcoholic is not the only person who needs healing; you do too!

My sister-in-law Eileen could not compete with the game of emotional chess my brother Glenn was playing, and she developed terrible stress and anxiety. She even developed severe physical symptoms from it all. Her full story is further down in this chapter.

There are several good reasons to learn about how addict-alcoholics manipulate you:

• When you allow yourself to be manipulated, you are enabling the addict-alcoholic.

Understanding what type of manipulation is being used, how it works, and how to appropriately respond gives you the ability to disempower the manipulation and stop enabling.

• Manipulation puts you in conflict with yourself.

When you are exposed to long-term manipulation, it causes you to constantly question your gut instinct (intuition) and even what your physical senses are telling you (what you see, smell, or hear). When it comes to dealing with your addict-alcoholic, you don't know what's true anymore even if there are obvious signs right in front of you.

• The ability to identify and disempower manipulation helps protect you from mental, emotional, and physical damage.

Long-term manipulation erodes your ability to trust, attacks your self-confidence, disconnects you from yourself and, shuts down your own intuition. The result for you is constant stress and that stress manifests in you as mental, emotional, and physical damage.

You may find yourself constantly irritable, depressed, or feeling hopeless. You may find it hard to sleep, hard to trust anybody, or hard to relax and have fun. You may lose your self-confidence and feel disconnected from what makes you happy. You lose connection to your own intuition. Even worse, all this emotional stress can manifest into physical symptoms.

I want to share another story with you which exemplifies the points above. At the beginning of this book, I introduced you to my oldest brother Glenn and his partner Eileen. This is Eileen's story. Eileen was together with Glenn at his worst as an active addict-alcoholic. Glenn manipulated Eileen badly during this time. Check out her story of what living with my addicted brother did to her.

I ask you to try to identify with what Eileen shares with you regardless of your relationship role with the addict-alcoholic in your life. Try to see where you are the same as Eileen. Especially when she reveals how the situation made her feel, ask yourself: "Have I experienced anything like this?"

* * *

Eileen's story of who she became from living with my addict-alcoholic brother:

"The left side of my face became paralyzed from the stress of living with Glenn."

Before dating Glenn, I was a person who was happy in life. I always look for the positive in people and situations. I was a relaxed, totally unsuspecting person.

I had known Glenn through mutual friends for many years before we dated. When we first started dating, he had just gotten out of rehab and was temporarily living with his parents. He seemed to be doing well.

In the beginning of our relationship Glenn was a thoughtful, loving, emotionally available guy. We had great times together and great conversations about life. We really connected.

After the first few months passed, things slowly started to happen which seemed out of character for him. He started to not answer my phone calls. He used to always answer my calls. When I asked him why he didn't answer my calls he would quickly come back with "My phone was dead" or "My phone was on silent."

When he would answer my calls, there were times when he didn't sound quite right to me. I couldn't put my finger on it; he wasn't slurring but there was something different about the way he spoke. One time I mustered up the courage to ask him why he sounded different, and he quickly answered, "My mouth is dry" or "I'm tired, I didn't sleep well last night."

We frequently went out to dinner on dates. At first, he was always at the restaurant waiting for me when I arrived, but then he started arriving late. One time he even nodded out in the middle of dinner. When I asked him if he was feeling OK, he said, "I took some antihistamines, and they made me drowsy."

I still really enjoyed being with Glenn. Pretty soon after we started dating, he moved in with me. As we were around each other much more now, I started to notice that sometimes he would be absolutely fine and other times he wasn't the usual Glenn I knew. It wasn't predictable.

As little incidents like this continued for the next year, I started to become very confused. Every time he seemed off and I had the courage to say something, he always had a plausible explanation. I started to think to myself: What the hell is going on?!

I began to suspect he might be drinking or using again. With that in mind I became hypervigilant and slowly began to uncover what he was really up to. I started to search through his things when he wasn't around. I remember one time I searched the trunk of his car and found a bottle of prescription pills stashed in his baseball bag. Mind you, he had not been on a baseball team for years, and the date on the prescription bottle was recent. I also began to check in with the local liquor store owner to see if he had been there. Sometimes the answer from the store owner was yes.

Every time I confronted him about what I discovered, he quickly presented me with a plausible alternative to what I thought was happening. He would get angry with me and his anger would cause me to back down. I started to question my own sense of reality. I began to lose touch with my intuition, my gut feelings.

Obsessive thinking took control of me. I turned into a private investigator on steroids. I was constantly trying to figure out what he was doing, where he was getting his drugs and alcohol, how much, with whom he was doing them, and how often.

Terrible stress and anxiety developed within me. The stress in turn manifested physically in the form of Bell's palsy. The left side of my face had become paralyzed from the stress of living with Glenn.

I also developed a deep sense of guilt and shame because I started lying to my family about him. I remember one Thanksgiving morning I lied to my family about not being able to join them. I told them I was sick when really, I was going to pick Glenn up at rehab. I was too embarrassed to have to tell them I was going to pick up my partner at rehab. As I was driving to pick him up, I distinctly remember having to use my index finger to blink my left eye because it wouldn't close due to the Bell's palsy.

I started to call my brother-in-law Craig to talk to him because he was in recovery and knew about addiction. Craig would have me describe the things Glenn was doing and saying to me. He would tell me what was really going on because he did those things too when he was an active addict-alcoholic. Craig confirmed what my gut instincts were telling me all along; things were not as Glenn was portraying. Even with Craig's sup-

port, it was very hard to navigate the situation and I felt sick to my stomach all the time. I became depressed.

After many conversations with Craig, I realized I was constantly being gaslighted. I realized Glenn also used anger to control me. I had lost touch with my intuition and didn't even trust my own eyes and ears. I had become as sick as Glenn was.

I hated the person I had become. I went against the things I believe in by lying to my family. I didn't feel good about searching through Glenn's things behind his back. My positivity was gone, and negative thinking took over. I was hypervigilant all the time, looking for bad signs from Glenn. I found it very difficult to be the relaxed person I used to be. The person I had become from living with Glenn was not me and it was exhausting. I was tired all the time.

We eventually had a family intervention with Glenn, and he went to rehab yet again. After he got out of rehab, I didn't allow him to move back in with me. He went to live at a sober house. With Glenn out of the house, my stress levels went back to normal, I wasn't feeling anxious all the time, and the Bell's palsy went away. I was relaxed again in my own home. My energy levels returned.

Glenn worked really hard at his recovery, and it showed. He returned to the Glenn I knew from when we first started dating. Despite his progress, it took me a long time to trust him again. After two years of Glenn working hard at his recovery, I felt good enough to allow him to move in with me again. Early on I was still hypervigilant around him. Every time he left the room, I would again wonder what he was up to. I once again found it difficult to feel relaxed in my own house with him around.

Today many years into this journey, things are much better. We have a trusting relationship. I am relaxed in my own house. I don't go against my own code of conduct (like lying). I am back to being the positive person I used to be. We have both worked hard at recovery, and it shows in our relationship which is better than it ever has been.

* * *

The addict-alcoholic's desired result of manipulation is that their loved ones become confused about reality, unable to recognize what is really going on. This enables the addict-alcoholic to keep using the way they are without being called out. Although the addict-alcoholic is only intending to protect their ability to use, for the loved ones like you the long-term manipulation places you in a tangled mess of emotions and twisted facts where nothing seems black and white.

Have you ever bristled at someone who made a comment to you about your addicted loved one which felt like a harsh judgment? To outsiders of the situation who have not been manipulated, the addict-alcoholic's problem and what they are doing to their loved ones is obvious. People who are beyond the reach of addict-alcoholic's manipulative influence can think clearly and are baffled by how the loved ones like you are not able to see the reality of the situation.

Here is a fact which might be difficult for you to accept:

Manipulation requires two people: One to manipulate (the addict-alcoholic) and one to allow themselves to be manipulated (you).

If you feel that you are being manipulated and you don't say anything, you are sending the silent message that you are a willing participant in their manipulation. When you show you are a willing participant, it sets the stage for more manipulation.

Addict-alcoholic manipulation is chronic; it's not a one-time deal. Recognizing and calling out manipulation isn't about blaming or judging; it's about fostering an environment that supports genuine recovery by promoting honesty, accountability, and healthy boundaries.

A key point here is even though your addict-alcoholic was manipulating only to protect their ability to use, and they weren't necessarily trying to damage you, the result is you have been subjected to chronic mind games, and it has absolutely damaged you. Again, this is one of the reasons why addiction is called a family disease. As we saw from Eileen's story, the mind games can even cause severe physical symptoms.

5.3 MANIPULATION IS NOT A PERSONAL INSULT TO YOU

Have you ever caught the addict-alcoholic in your life in a shameless lie or some other type of manipulation and felt disgusted they could do such a thing? Did you ever find out about a revealing piece of information and feel like an idiot for not seeing the truth behind their lie?

Their manipulation is not a personal insult even though what they say or do may be very personal and very insulting. They don't manipulate because they don't respect you or they don't love you. The addict-alcoholic manipulates you to protect their ability to use.

Also, please know this:

You are not the only target for the addict-alcoholic's manipulation!

They will manipulate absolutely anybody who stands in their way of using or has something they want (such as money, drugs, or medications in their medicine cabinet). Nobody is off limits: spouses, children, grandparents, doctors, neighbors, work colleagues, or store owners. They would even manipulate the family dog if it would get them something to feed their addiction. Believe it or not, I have heard real life stories from addict-alcoholics who brought their pet to the veterinarian and pretended the pet was in pain to get pain medication. The veterinarian can't just ask the cat what level of pain it's experiencing!

Love the person, challenge the disease. Challenge the disease by recognizing manipulation and not taking it personally.

Remember, for an addict-alcoholic, manipulation becomes autonomic like breathing. When the addict-alcoholic manipulates, they may not be consciously thinking, *I am going to manipulate this person now.* So, try not to take their manipulation personally, even when what they say or do is very personal! When you take their manipulation personally, you become even more entangled in it.

The addict-alcoholic's manipulation has nothing to do with you or anyone else; it is only to protect their ability to use the way they need to.

CHAPTER 6:

How Manipulation Works

Let's begin this chapter with a story from Michael, a sibling to an addict-alcoholic.

* * *

Michael's story about his alcoholic brother:

"He manipulated me to the point where I no longer believed my own eyes and ears."

My oldest brother struggled with addiction and caused a lot of turmoil in the family. When he wasn't around, the conversation always migrated to him and how bad things were. When we were with him, we were always on high alert.

Every time I saw him, I would look for signs he had been using. I would first watch the way he walked. As he got closer, I would inspect his eyes. Then I would listen carefully to the way he spoke. I was constantly asking myself, "Is he drunk or high?" Since he was almost always using, I had no real sober baseline for comparison. When I thought he had been using, it was hard to decide whether to say anything. I didn't want to accuse him of using if he hadn't.

There were times when I was pretty sure he had been using. It still took a lot of courage to confront him about it, especially in the moment. He always seemed to have a quick excuse or seemingly valid reason for his behavior. Even though deep down I knew he wasn't sober, I would end up doubting what my own eyes and ears were telling me.

I remember one day I interacted with him when he clearly had not used yet. The difference in his personality was stark. His walk was different, his eyes were clear, and his speech was impeccable. It became apparent to me that all those other times I thought he wasn't sober I was spot on.

I realized all his excuses and false reasoning had manipulated me to the point where I no longer believed my own eyes and ears. He succeeded in causing me to doubt myself. I was amazed at how much my ability to properly assess his state had been impaired by self-doubt. My self-doubt in turn took away my confidence to confront him.

Here is the real crazy part of this story: I am a sober addict-alcoholic in recovery, and I too had been a master manipulator. My brother succeeded in manipulating me, a former master manipulator! This experience showed me how emotionally tangled the loved ones can get when a family member is an addict-alcoholic. Even when they have intellectual knowledge concerning the disease of addiction, they still get tangled in the emotional web of manipulation an addict-alcoholic weaves.

I realized the loved ones become incapable of seeing what is right in front of them and need help too. I sought support through my network of recovery friends, and they helped me navigate the situation in a healthy way.

6.1 INTRODUCTION

In chapter five, I described the "why" behind addict-alcoholic manipulation and its effects on you. In this chapter, I will describe in general how manipulation works. Michael's story demonstrates how even a small amount of self-doubt cracks the door open for an addict-alcoholic to manipulate. Creating self-doubt and causing you to question yourself is only one way an addict-alcoholic can control you. There are other ways at their disposal which we will discuss.

6.2 HOW ADDICT-ALCOHOLIC MANIPULATION WORKS

The addict-alcoholic manipulates you by:

1. discouraging open and factual discussions,
2. keeping details and facts hidden, and
3. persuading you to tolerate behavior you normally would not tolerate.

You are going to see the word *tolerate* a lot in this chapter, so let's define it. According to the Merriam-Webster dictionary:

Tolerate:

1. to allow to be or to be done **without prohibition, hindrance, or contradiction**[7]

Tolerating behavior does not mean you agree with the behavior, or you do not express dissatisfaction; it means you do not deliver sufficient consequences to prevent the behavior from happening again.

If you say to your addict-alcoholic, "I am not going to tolerate this behavior," and it happens again, then what? Maybe you don't talk to them for a few days? Maybe you hold on to your anger for a week and make life unpleasant for them?

Addict-alcoholics push the boundaries of acceptable behavior to the extreme. Frequently anything short of "ultimatum" level consequences will not prevent them from again doing what they always do.

I have heard a quote which describes your role in this relationship with an addicted loved one perfectly:

"What you tolerate, you encourage."

When you tolerate unacceptable behavior, you find yourself in the same situations with them over and over: feeling resentful, hopeless, angry, worried, lonely, and depressed once again.

---

7 "tolerate." *Merriam-Webster.com.* 2025. https://www.merriam-webster.com.

6.3 THE WAYS MANIPULATION CONTROLS YOU

There are countless ways that addicts manipulate their loved ones and even themselves. The main ways the addict-alcoholic in your life manipulates and controls you are shown in the diagram below:

1) Manipulation makes you question yourself.

- Have you ever spoken up to the addict-alcoholic in your life about their using and their response created some doubt in your mind?
- Have they ever said something like, "It's not what you think it is," and made you question what you saw, heard, or smelled?

- Did your gut instinct ever tell you something wasn't right, and they came up with some excuse which made you feel like maybe your gut feeling was wrong?

If the addict-alcoholic can knock you off balance mentally and emotionally, you will begin to question your own observations and intuition.

Mentally, one way addict-alcoholics cause you to question yourself is to directly deny your observations. Your addict-alcoholic, a person you love, want to trust, and want to believe in, feeds you misinformation. Your loved one is lying to you, and it breaks your heart to believe it. So, you try not to believe it but that conflicts with what your eyes and ears are telling you. You end up confused. When you become confused, they control you even more.

Emotionally, when the addict-alcoholic knocks you off balance, you feel insecure and doubt yourself. The insecurity and self-doubt then take away your courage, fortitude, and energy to confront them. Addict-alcoholics can create emotional insecurity by evoking sympathy through guilt trips or making you feel bad about yourself.

It does not take much for the addict-alcoholic to make you question yourself. In the court of law, to be convicted a person must be proven guilty "*beyond a reasonable doubt.*" In the "emotional court of the household," your addict-alcoholic is their own defense lawyer and all they need to do is plant the tiniest seed of doubt for you to question yourself.

Caring for an addicted loved one who consistently manipulates is mentally and emotionally exhausting.

When they do this over the course of months or years, your ability to accurately assess a situation based on facts and intuition becomes impaired. You end up tolerating more and more unacceptable behavior.

2) Manipulation influences and controls your perception of reality.

- Did you ever catch the addict-alcoholic drunk or high and their response downplayed or minimized the situation?
- Have they ever tried to make you think an incident was not what you thought it was, or as bad as you thought?
- Have they ever implied you overreacted?

When the addict-alcoholic can influence your perception, they can control your assessments and opinions of any situation which involves them. This helps them avoid getting in trouble, being called out for their behavior or at the very least gets you to tolerate their behavior.

When the addict-alcoholic influences your perception, they control your assessments and opinions of any situation which involves them. This helps them avoid getting in trouble, being called out for their behavior, or at the very least gets you to tolerate their behavior.

Here are a few ways they do this.

- They can downplay situations where they got drunk or high.
- They can exaggerate situations if it suits their purpose. For example, they can hype up an event ahead of time, laying the foundation to make it seem OK for them to drink or use. They can use a positive spin like, "I am so

excited to see my friends again; it has been a while since we all partied together."

- Or, they can take the negative angle by saying, "It has been such a stressful time lately; I just want to go out, have some fun and relax for once." Maybe the addict-alcoholic really isn't that stressed out, but they coax you into perceiving that they are.

They do these things because they know you don't like it when they drink or use. To combat that, they influence how you perceive situations so you will tolerate their using.

When it comes to influencing your perception of reality, they have many ways to do it.

3) Manipulation keeps details and facts hidden from you.

- When you are with the addict-alcoholic at a gathering, do they spend much of the time out of your sight line (such as staying in a different room than you at the party)?
- Did you ever feel like the addict-alcoholic was hiding something from you?
- Has the addict-alcoholic ever left your sight to perform a task, and it seemed to take longer than it should have?
- Does the addict-alcoholic frequently tell you they need some "alone time"?
- Has someone else ever revealed details concerning the addict-alcoholic which the addict-alcoholic neglected to tell you? Have you ever said to the addict-alcoholic, "You never told me this"?

- Have you ever gone out with the addict-alcoholic (out to eat or to a gathering), you didn't see them drink or use that much, but they still became very drunk or high?
- When you are out to eat with the addict-alcoholic, do they repeatedly leave your sight, such as go to the bathroom frequently or go out to the car to get something they "forgot"?

Addict-alcoholics will keep potentially incriminating details and facts hidden as much as possible, so any assessment you might make is based on incomplete information.

One common way they do this is to physically hide themselves from you. That way, you don't see them drinking or using. A classic one I did myself and have heard over and over in recovery meetings is they invent reasons to leave the room (like to go to the bathroom). When they are out of sight from you, they can chug from a hidden bottle of alcohol or pop some pills they have in their pocket.

Keeping details and facts about their using hidden from you enables them to dispute anything you say because you don't have hard proof.

4) Manipulation gets you to back down.

- Have you ever caught the addict-alcoholic high or drunk, their excuse caught you off guard, and you didn't know what to say so you just dropped the subject?
- Has the addict-alcoholic ever become very angry when you asked them about their using?

The addict-alcoholic doesn't need you to believe their excuses or agree with them, they just need the confrontation to stop. Whether it's ridiculous excuses, angry outbursts, or any other technique, they get you to back down from pursuing any discussions concerning their using.

5) Manipulation distracts you by changing the subject.

- Have you ever called the addict-alcoholic out on their behavior, and at the end of the conversation the topic had totally changed?
- When you call them out, do they ever respond by pointing out your shortcomings and the conversation ends up focused on you?

Changing the subject is an age-old diversion technique. The addict-alcoholic will try to change the subject when you call them out on their behavior, their substance abuse problem, or any other incident which has to do with their using.

Their goal is to shift the discussion to a new topic long enough to distract you away from their using. Sometimes I would use this tact even when I wasn't in trouble. If my wife was getting close to a sensitive spot, I would make sure to steer her away from my vulnerability.

Most addict-alcoholics are very good at smoothly changing the subject. They are experts at transitioning attention away from them and onto someone or something else.

6) Manipulation softens your behavioral boundary lines.

- Have you ever witnessed the addict-alcoholic in your life drink too much and when you commented, they responded with something like, "It's been a tough week; I just want to relax"?

The question I have for you is this:

When is it OK for them to drink or use heavily?

If your answer is never, then you have a definitive black-and-white behavioral boundary line. The addict-alcoholic will try to soften your behavioral boundary with emotional pleas or other manipulation techniques.

Addict-alcoholics get you to soften your behavioral boundary lines on an incident-by-incident basis. They convince you in the moment to make a "one time" exception to your code of conduct. When they soften your behavioral boundary lines, they get you to tolerate their behavior. Remember the definition of tolerance at the beginning of this section? It means you put up with their behavior, even though you still think it's unacceptable.

Here is how softening your boundary lines can happen:

Your first comment focused on their drinking and how it makes you feel. You stated your truth. Second, with one little comment they exploit your close relationship with them and try to evoke sympathy from you. Third, their emotional appeal is successful because you love them. Your sympathy shifts your focus away from their drinking or using and onto feeling bad for them. Because you feel bad for them, you grant an exception and soften your previously defined behavioral boundary.

Even if the addict-alcoholic did have a tough week (say, they lost their job), does that make it OK for them to drink or use heavily?

Your answer may still be no; however, since they evoked sympathy from you, maybe you let them do it this one time. This is what I mean by "tolerating behavior" versus "accepting behavior." You still may not think their drinking or using is OK (you still think it's unacceptable), but you put up with it anyway (you tolerate it).

7) Manipulation shifts your standards for tolerable behavior.

- Have you ever been mad at yourself for what you put up with from the addict-alcoholic?
- Have you ever taken a good look at what you put up with now and realized you now tolerate behavior from the addict-alcoholic which you never would have put up with months, years, or decades ago?
- Have you ever looked at the mess the situation has become and asked yourself, "How did I get here?"

One by one, each little manipulative incident from them persuades you to tolerate a little more. In time, situations which you never would have put up with months or years ago become regular occurrences that now carry no consequences for the addict-alcoholic.

Your behavioral boundary lines migrate so slowly that you don't notice.

If you have ever thought to yourself "How did I get here?" the diagram below shows you how.

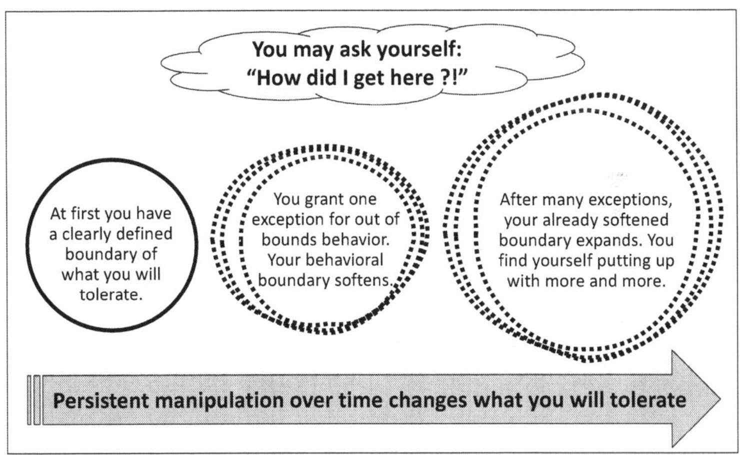

As I worked on this project of "becoming the secret decoder ring" for you, the loved ones of addict-alcoholics, I sat down and talked to many loved ones of addict-alcoholics. It became clear to me that "shifting your standards for tolerable behavior" is a common occurrence for loved ones like you. Sometimes you are not consciously aware of it. Other times you are aware of it, but the changes are so small it doesn't seem like a big deal in the moment.

Your behavioral boundary lines migrate so slowly, you may not notice it's happening.

In actuality, when you grant an exception to their behavior, any small exception whatsoever, it is a big deal. Your small exceptions now become the new behavioral boundary. Addict-alcoholics soften and shift your behavioral boundary lines one small inch at a time. They break it down into bite-sized pieces with many little incidents, so you don't notice your boundary shifting.

When the addict-alcoholic gets you to tolerate what your gut instinct says you shouldn't, it creates an inner conflict in you. This inner conflict can cause you to lose sleep, be constantly irritable, and it becomes a source of anger, frustration, and resentment for people like you.

The next section will shed more light on this subject.

6.4 HOW DO THEY GET YOU TO TOLERATE THEIR BEHAVIOR?

Every person has a set of values which define their personal boundaries for acceptable and unacceptable behavior (your "code of conduct"). These values come from your upbringing, spiritual beliefs, or other sources of positive influence. They are your core guiding principles by which you live.

Before active addiction took hold of your loved one, any behavior which violated your code of conduct was deemed unacceptable and you didn't tolerate it. You either said something in the moment to state your disapproval, or you silently stated your truth by distancing yourself from the situation; you refused to participate.

As active addiction takes hold of your loved one, they systematically manipulate your behavioral boundary lines. Over months and years, they slowly shift your code of conduct. The result is you put up with more and more.

Has the addict-alcoholic in your life ever defended their behavior by pointing out somebody who was worse? When the addict-alcoholic knows their current behavior is unacceptable to you, one way they try to minimize the trouble they get in is to divert your attention onto something worse. By making these comparisons to worse people or incidents, the addict-alcoholic grooms you to change your code of conduct for tolerable behavior. Over time you have been persuaded to tolerate the unacceptable. You slowly permit more behavior that you don't like.

Blame-shifting and scapegoating are common ways to avoid taking responsibility for their behavior.

Sometimes the addict-alcoholic has one particular incident which is really bad, a "blow out." After the blow-out incident, they can point to it as the new benchmark by which all future incidents should be compared. They might say something like, "At least I wasn't as bad as that other time."

In short, they minimize their current behavior by pointing out it is not as bad as someone else's behavior or their own "blow-out" incident.

Here is a key point:

When they shift your code of conduct it does not mean you approve of the behavior; it just means you tolerate it. The result is the addict-alcoholic does not suffer sufficient consequences to prevent them from repeating.

Reflecting on what you tolerate, do you find yourself putting up with repetitive behavior you don't like? If you answered yes, know almost all loved ones of addict-alcoholics experience this. The shifting of your behavioral boundaries happens one small inch at a time and is a consequence of living with an addict-alcoholic.

Boiling a frog

Have you ever heard of the analogy of "boiling a frog"? It goes something like this:

If you take a frog from its pond and try to put it into a pot of boiling water, it will immediately try to jump out. Now take a frog and put it in a pot of water the same temperature as the pond. The frog stays in the pot no problem. Then, if the pot is slowly heated to a boil, the frog does not notice the temperature is rising and eventually finds itself in boiling water, slowly coming to its demise.

The analogy depicts how slow, small changes over time may be imperceptible or, if you do notice, it's such a small change that it doesn't seem like a big deal and an exception is made. This is a good example of how chronic manipulation slowly gets you to tolerate things you previously would not. In the case of the frog, it is ultimately deadly. In the case of your relationship with the addict-alcoholic, it is connection and trust which are killed.

When you compromise your boundaries over time, you inadvertently create a safety net for the addict-alcoholic to continue using, which is enabling. They can shift your code of conduct reactively or proactively.

Reactively:

They try to influence your criteria for tolerable behavior in the moment they are caught. They compare their behavior to another person's worse behavior or their own past event which was worse. Their defense to you calling them out might be something like, "Last night I wasn't as bad as I was at the New Year's party."

When caught, the addict-alcoholic is very good at making up this type of rationale in the moment to get you to back down.

Proactively:

They try to shift your behavioral boundary before anything even happens. One way to do this is to try influencing your expectations of a future event.

Let's say you are going to a party with your addict-alcoholic partner, where he will see one of his old friends he hasn't seen in a while. Before you go, he may say something like:

"Bill is coming to the party tonight, and I haven't seen him in a while. He is going to want to have some fun and drink; he always gets insanely drunk."

His short statement is packed with manipulative implications, so let's break it down:

1) Even if you do not approve of their using, the addict-alcoholic claims he has good reason to drink at the party because he hasn't seen Bill in a long time. This sets the stage for them to at least have some alcohol.

2) Since it is Bill who likes to party, Bill will be leading the way, and the addict-alcoholic shouldn't be held accountable for what happens. The implication is they will just be a follower, a victim of circumstance.

3) Here comes the comparison: because Bill "always gets insanely drunk," even if your addict-alcoholic also gets drunk it probably won't be as bad as Bill. The implied message is whatever happens with your addict-alcoholic, it should be tolerated because Bill is worse.

4) The loved one should probably plan on driving home because the addict-alcoholic will be intoxicated.

So, before you even go to the party, the addict-alcoholic's overall message is your behavioral boundary should be softened and their potential behavior at the party should be tolerated. On top of that, you should plan to drive their drunk butt home from the party because they have basically implied that they won't be able to drive.

6.5 ADDICT-ALCOHOLICS ALSO BREAK THEIR OWN CODE OF CONDUCT

Addict-alcoholics don't only shift the code of conduct of their loved ones through manipulation, they also do it to themselves. David's story in section 3.6 titled "At least I wasn't taking the 5's" demonstrates this.

When David was stealing the one-dollar bills, he told himself, "At least I wasn't taking the 5's." He self-justified taking his sister's money *by making up a worse situation in his own mind. He manipulated himself!*

Addict-alcoholics create self-delusions which enable them to believe their behavior is "not that bad." This lessens any personal guilt or negative feelings about their using and how it affects their loved ones. David's story is a great example of this.

If they break their own code of conduct, how could they possibly live by yours?!

6.6 THE MANY WAYS ADDICT-ALCOHOLICS MANIPULATE

- Have you ever started a conversation with the addict-alcoholic in your life about their using, but when the conversation was over you felt like you got nowhere?
- Have you ever felt guilty after calling out the addict-alcoholic on their using, and thought maybe you were too hard on them?
- Have you ever felt like you weren't getting the whole story from the addict-alcoholic?
- Have you ever been angry at the addict-alcoholic for a particular incident and, after discussing it with them, you felt like you misinterpreted or misremembered the incident?
- Have you looked around at what your relationship with the addict-alcoholic has become and asked yourself, "How did I get here?"
- Have you ever called out the addict-alcoholic and their angry response made you drop the subject?

To prevent being caught or called out on their drinking or using, addict-alcoholics must become very good at assessing situations in real-time, thinking quickly on their feet, and manipulating you to defend their ability to use. The ways they are able to manipulate you are many. This is where my book title *Beyond the Lies* comes from!

Addict-alcoholics unconsciously hone the skill of quickly shifting to a different way of controlling you if one type of manipulation doesn't work. This means if you catch them manipulating and call them out, they may immediately move on to another tact.

To show how this can play out, let's expand upon the scenario from the diagram in section 6.3 titled "The addict-alcoholic starts to drink heavily and…." In this hypothetical but very realistic scenario, the addict-alcoholic is leaving work on a Friday evening…

Addict-alcoholic: As they leave work, they convince themself that it had been a tough week and that they deserve to get drunk. Knowing you won't tolerate them having more than say one or two drinks (which won't accomplish what the addict-alcoholic wants), they stop at a store, get alcohol, and drink it while they drive home.

You: When the addict-alcoholic walks in the door, you are pretty sure you smell alcohol on them. You debate to yourself whether to say anything because you don't want to fight. You decide to say something and in the most non-accusatory manner possible you ask, "Have you been drinking?"

Addict-alcoholic: "No, why do you ask?"

You: "Because you smell like alcohol."

Addict-alcoholic: "Well, my co-workers asked me to go for a few drinks after work with them."

You: "I love you but it's not OK when you drink like this."

Addict-alcoholic: "It's been a tough week; I just want to relax. What's wrong with that?"

You think to yourself: I guess it's OK this time.

This short interaction is absolutely packed with manipulation. It demonstrates how quickly addict-alcoholics think on their feet and shift their tactics. Let's analyze the above scenario and label what exactly happened. The manipulation tactics appear in bold capital letters on the right. Note how many times you see the bold print.

Addict-alcoholic: As they leave work, they convince themself that it had been a tough week and that they deserve to get drunk. Knowing you won't tolerate them having more than say one or two drinks (which won't accomplish what the addict-alcoholic wants), they stop at a store, get alcohol, and drink it while they drive home.

The addict-alcoholic's delusionary thinking convinces them they "deserve" to drink. They know that you won't tolerate it, so they **HIDE** it by drinking before they get home. Note their delusionary thinking also convinces them it is OK to drink while driving.

You: When the addict-alcoholic walks in the door, you are pretty sure you smell alcohol on them. You debate to yourself whether to say anything because you don't want to fight. You decide to say something and in the most non-accusatory manner possible you ask,
"Have you been drinking?"

You pay attention to what your five senses are telling you: you smelled alcohol. After a short debate with yourself you decide to say something. You ask a simple question in the most non-accusatory way possible.

Addict-alcoholic: "No, why do you ask?"

They answer "no," a **LIE** and then **DIRECTLY CHALLENGE** you by asking you to state your case..

You: "Because you smell like alcohol."

You have proof, your sense of smell. You listen to your senses and state what you observe., catching them in their lie.

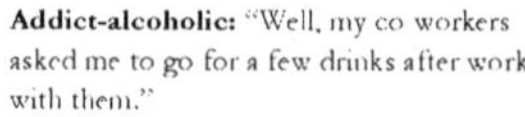

Addict-alcoholic: "Well, my co workers asked me to go for a few drinks after work with them."

They see they are caught immediately shift tact. They **LIE** again saying co workers asked them to go. Note this also an **EXCUSE** why they drank, implying it wasn't their idea to drink, it was their co worker's. Their fabricated scenario also **MINIMIZES** the seriousness of what they did because it implies that they didn't drink alone while driving home. Furthermore, they **MINIMIZE** their drinking again by using the term "a few drinks," making it sound like no big deal.

You: "I love you but it's not OK when you drink like this."

You do the right thing, you don't get caught up in the details of why they drank, with whom or how much. You simply state your truth..

Addict-alcoholic: "It's been a tough week; I just want to relax. What's wrong with that"

They use a **JUSTIFICATION** by saying it was a tough week. This is also a **GUILT TRIP;** you should feel sorry for them and allow them to drink without criticism. They then **FLIP THE FOCUS** back on you, implying that you are over-reacting by saying "what's wrong with that?".

You think to yourself: "I guess it's OK this time."

After stating your truth multiple times, their continued manipulative comments wear you down. You allow your truth (you don't like it when they drink) to be pushed aside.

In this short conversation, the addict-alcoholic used ten manipulative tactics! By seamlessly transitioning from one tactic to another and yet another, they lead you in circles until you stop pursuing the discussion or, at the very least, the subject matter is no longer about their drinking and drugging. They redirect the confrontation to other topics with ease and this is why you felt like you got nowhere, because it became a different conversation from what you started with. This scenario finishes with the addict-alcoholic flipping the focus onto you, making you the topic of the conversation instead of their drinking.

> Addict-alcoholic manipulation goes way "beyond the lies."

The collateral damage is that people like you end up doubting yourself, feeling anxious, and feeling isolated. Even though they were only doing it to protect their ability to use, the result is you have been subjected to systematic psychological and emotional warfare which has made you sick.

After reading *Beyond the Lies*, maybe the scenario above would not have ended with you thinking, I guess it's OK this time, allowing their manipulation to work. Perhaps it would have ended with you taking your power back and saying,

"I get it. You certainly have had a tough week. Let me know how I can support you in any way other than watching you drink. Your drinking is still not OK with me."

6.7 SO, THEY ADMITTED TO THEIR PROBLEM, WHAT HAPPENS NOW?

- How can admitting to their problem be manipulation?
- Has the addict-alcoholic in your life admitted to their problem?
- If so, did you feel immediate relief hoping things will finally change?
- If they admitted to their problem, what happened *after*?
- Did they get sober, and now everything is rainbows and butterflies?
- Or did the addict-alcoholic take small steps to address their problem (perhaps to appease you) but they are still drinking or using? If so, how does this make you feel?

Addict-alcoholics will use every manipulation tactic possible before getting to the point where they admit to their problem. Admitting to an addiction can be incredibly difficult due to a combination of psychological, social, and emotional factors. They will only admit to their problem when they are left with no other options. This is because if they admit to their problem, they will have to do something about it. They may not be ready to give up drinking and drugging just yet, and they will exhaust all options to protect their ability to continue drinking and using.

Hitting an outside bottom (such as losing their license or getting fired from work) sometimes provides undeniable evidence which burns a hole through their delusional thinking, and they finally admit to themselves there is a substance abuse problem. See section 3.15 for discussion on outside bottoms if you want to revisit what that means.

The question is:

What happens* after *they admit to their problem?

Robert's stories about his alcoholic mother in sections 3.16 and 4.5 show what frequently happens. Once the addict-alcoholic finally admits to their problem, almost all the loved ones feel a sense of relief and may think: *Finally! We can move on from this.* Unfortunately, most addict-alcoholics do not turn the corner for good after they admit to their problem. The reason for this is most addict-alcoholics admit to their problem in a state of compliance instead of surrender; the circumstances they are caught in are undeniable, so they admit to it because they have no other choice. Just because they agree to go to rehab or do something about their problem, it doesn't mean they

Most addict-alcoholics admit to their problem in a state of compliance instead of surrender.

have surrendered. Revisit section 3.16 for the discussion on compliance versus surrender. In a state of compliance, they may admit to their problem just to get you (or the judge, their boss, or the police) off their back in the moment, which is manipulation.

On a positive note, admitting to their problem is the most important step to begin the journey toward recovery. The journey is usually filled with smooth and bumpy periods, with progress followed by regression backward. The journey is not linear.

During their journey the addict-alcoholic can and will still use manipulation on you. Working at getting sober brings up a lot of fear, and manipulation is a protection mechanism which they have learned all too well. The good news is as they progress through the different stages toward physical and emotional sobriety, their fear starts to wane. Consequently, their tendency to try to manipulate you typically also wanes.

6.8 REFLECTIONS: HOW MUCH HAVE YOU BEEN MANIPULATED?

Thinking back on your situation, check any boxes you relate to. If you check more than one box, maybe you should take a closer look at how much you are being manipulated.

- ☐ Has the addict-alcoholic ever caused you to question yourself, especially something your five senses told you (they smelled like alcohol, they sounded like they slurred, their eyes looked dopey)?
- ☐ Have they ever influenced your perception of "reality," convincing you to think you observed things wrong, or you overreacted? Name a specific incident you remember.

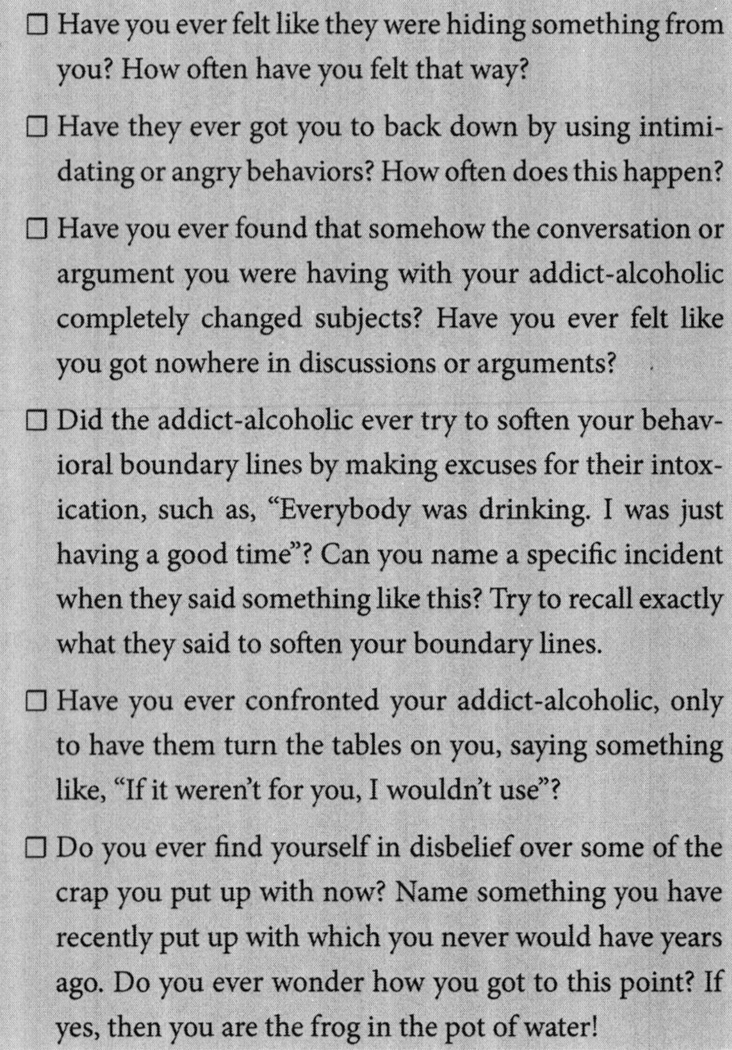

- ☐ Have you ever felt like they were hiding something from you? How often have you felt that way?
- ☐ Have they ever got you to back down by using intimidating or angry behaviors? How often does this happen?
- ☐ Have you ever found that somehow the conversation or argument you were having with your addict-alcoholic completely changed subjects? Have you ever felt like you got nowhere in discussions or arguments?
- ☐ Did the addict-alcoholic ever try to soften your behavioral boundary lines by making excuses for their intoxication, such as, "Everybody was drinking. I was just having a good time"? Can you name a specific incident when they said something like this? Try to recall exactly what they said to soften your boundary lines.
- ☐ Have you ever confronted your addict-alcoholic, only to have them turn the tables on you, saying something like, "If it weren't for you, I wouldn't use"?
- ☐ Do you ever find yourself in disbelief over some of the crap you put up with now? Name something you have recently put up with which you never would have years ago. Do you ever wonder how you got to this point? If yes, then you are the frog in the pot of water!

6.9 WHAT EFFECT DOES MANIPULATION HAVE ON YOU?

In section 4.6 "What does enabling addict-alcoholics mean?", you were introduced to my friend Maria with her teenage son who was an addict. Let's hear more of her story.

* * *

Maria's story of having an addict teenage son:

"I was constantly replaying his whole life, trying to find where I screwed up."

I am the proud mother of four children. Before addiction came into my household, I was an upbeat person, always looked for the positive in everything; I trusted my children 100%. I was not an overly strict mother; however, I made sure I instilled good values in them. All my kids were great kids. Caring, respectful, responsible; everything a parent could hope for. My relationships with my children were great and we had mutual respect. I was confident and on top of the world.

My oldest son had it all going for him. He was smart, popular, athletic, and good looking. He was laid back, kind, and easy to get along with. He had a magnetic personality and was a leader. I had a very open, close, and wonderful relationship with him. Of my four kids, he was the last one I thought I would have trouble with.

When he was fourteen years old, I noticed he began to change. He started staying in his room a lot. He began to withdraw from interacting with me and the rest of the family. I thought it was just his age and hormones.

One day, I went to his room to try to reconnect with him and see what was going on. As I lovingly poked at him about what was up with him, he started crying. He said he was sad; he felt like no one liked him, and he was a failure. He was acting highly insecure. He had never been like this before.

We decided to take him to a psychiatrist. They told us he was anxious and depressed. They prescribed him antidepressants. Unfortunately, the medication seemed to make him worse. He became even more anxious, depressed, and withdrawn.

I really didn't know what was going on with him. I thought he was going through a major teenage hormonal crisis. He continued to stay in his bedroom, slept all the time, and did not participate in any family activities. He even slept through Christmas dinner that year.

Then he started becoming aggressive. He would yell at me in ways he never came close to before. He made me feel like I was responsible for the troubles he was having. He also started getting into trouble with the police. It became a weekly occurrence for the police to show up at our house. I of course immediately came to my son's defense as any mother would. I yelled at the police (something I thought I would never do) and told them to stop harassing my son.

In the middle of one night, I was awakened by him fumbling around in the basement. When I went downstairs and asked him what he was doing, he turned and just started screaming at me. He was swearing at me, calling me terrible names. I was shocked. He had never spoken to me like this before. He took his backpack and stormed out of the house. I felt like I was in some alternate reality; nothing was making sense to me. I was starting to suspect maybe he was on drugs.

On another night, a car pulled up in front of the house and he went out there to meet whoever was in the car. The car was there for less than thirty seconds and then drove away. As I watched, my intuition was telling me drugs had entered my son's life. I knew with all my heart he had just done a drug deal.

This was a turning point for me. When my son came back in, I asked what that was all about and he nonchalantly said, "It was just my friend. He was dropping something off." I was afraid to ask him if it was drugs because of how volatile he had become, so I didn't say anything more.

He had a total personality change. The kid I was living with was not the kid I knew just a few short months ago.

The worry and stress with my oldest son created constant tension in the house. The entire family became focused on whether he was home or not, what he was up to, what mood he was in, and if there was going to be yelling tonight. This all started to put tremendous strain on my relationship with my husband. I wanted someone to be angry at and blame, as he did, so we got angry with each other, wondering if the other could have done something to prevent this. We were constantly bickering and disagreeing on how to handle the situation. I wanted to do tough love, and I felt he was enabling our son by being too soft.

My son's emotional state became so bad that he revealed he wanted to kill himself by jumping off a cliff in town. I felt responsible and horribly guilty for what my son had become. The emotional stress I was feeling took its toll on me. I had trouble focusing at work, I wasn't giving any of my other three kids the attention they deserved, I stopped going out with my friends, and I was exhausted all the time.

Our son started getting into repeated trouble with police; eventually he was court ordered to go to rehab.

We ended up sending him to rehab. My hopes soared. We were hopeful that receiving the help he needed would give us back the wonderful person we knew him to be.

When he went to rehab, I knew he was safe, and I felt like I could breathe for the first time in a long time. My stress levels went back to normal. I felt like somebody stuck me with a pin and relieved the pressure. Without worrying about him all the time, I came back to life. My old self returned fast; I was more alive at work, more engaged with my family, and I was going out with my friends again. I felt like I had a new lease on life.

When he got out of rehab and came home, he seemed to be physically sober, but he still wasn't his old self. I found myself on high alert once again. Then my worst fears came true: I started seeing the same old signs he was using again. Whenever I got the courage to confront him, he always seemed to have an explanation for what was going on, making me think things were not what I thought they were. I would ask him why his eyes were so red, and he would just say he was tired. Sometimes he would guilt trip me with "You're my mother, I thought you were on my side, I can't believe you think I'm using again."

Turns out my intuition was right. He wasn't himself because he was still using. We had to send him to rehab again. It was a roller coaster ride. When he was at home, I was an anxious, hypervigilant wreck. It was exhausting. When he was in rehab, I returned to my old self. I felt like I was going crazy.

After he got out of the second rehab, he still wasn't himself, and the cycle started all over again. I became dark, anxious, and withdrawn; I didn't want to talk to anyone. I hid like a snail because I felt like a complete failure as a mother and didn't want to be judged. I stopped going out with friends. I withdrew to my room and lay in bed.

It wasn't just me. The whole family became focused on him. All we did was talk about him 24/7. "Where is he now? Does he seem OK today? Is he still sleeping? If he is, that's not good. What time was he supposed to be home? He's late and that's not good." Our other children got zero attention from their father and me.

As I lay in bed, I was constantly replaying his whole life, trying to find where I screwed up. I thought this whole thing was my fault; the guilt was overwhelming. I hated myself.

Then the miracle happened. One day he became so disgusted with himself and what he had become, he checked himself into rehab with no involvement from my husband and me. He hired a ride to rehab and didn't even tell us. Once I was able to speak to him, he told me he knew if he didn't give it his all, he would die. He did everything they told him to do and more. He worked hard at recovery while he was there.

When he got out of rehab this time, I saw the difference in him immediately. I got my son back! Another great sign was once out of rehab, he was still doing all the things they told him to do. He changed who he hung out with and where he went. He got back into exercise and sports. He attended recovery meetings.

As he got better, so did I. The anxiety went away. I once again returned to my old energetic, positive, social self. I still have moments of guilt, thinking I should have been able to prevent it all from happening, but as I heal, those moments happen less and less.

Reflecting back, I also want to say that the psychiatrist we went to really tried to help my son. They didn't fail us. The help they provided didn't work because my son wasn't being honest; he never revealed he was using drugs. How could they possibly help him if my son wouldn't be honest with them?

* * *

So, could you relate to anything Maria shared in her story?

One key dynamic I want to point out concerning Maria's son is the concept discussed in section 3.16: "Compliance versus surrender." When he went to the psychiatrist and to rehab the first two times, he participated from a state of compliance. His parents made him go. As a result, he was not open to the help being provided to him. Compliance has a shelf life so of course he ended up using again. The last time he went to rehab, he had entered a state of surrender where he became open to receiving help and it showed.

One theme I have heard from many of the loved ones of addict-alcoholics like you is that they at times feel like they are going crazy, and they stop trusting their own observations and intuition. They become hypervigilant, looking for the next bad thing to happen, and they are exhausted all the time. Can you relate to any of that?

Living with an active addict or alcoholic inevitably leaves a mark—no one remains unaffected.

Remember, even if your loved one is a high-functioning addict-alcoholic (successful at work, takes care of their chores around the house, no trouble with the law), the effect their disease of addiction has on you is most likely still profound. It is virtually impossible to go through the experience of living with an active addict-alcoholic without being affected. You likely have sustained some psychological, emotional, financial, and sometimes physical damage from your experience.

Moreover, as we discussed in section 4.1, "The identified patient," all the attention is usually on the dysfunction of the addict-alcoholic, and the effect on the loved ones is usually overlooked. The loved ones like you don't realize you also need to heal from their disease of addiction.

If you had difficulty relating to Maria's story, I have more questions for you in the next section!

6.10 REFLECTIONS: HOW HAS MANIPULATION AFFECTED YOU?

How many of the questions below can you answer yes to?

- ☐ Have you ever doubted what you saw, heard, or smelled, finally deciding it wasn't what you thought it was?
- ☐ Have you completely lost trust in the addict-alcoholic?
- ☐ Have you ever felt ashamed and blamed yourself for everything that's going on?
- ☐ Have you lost the confidence to stand up for yourself?
- ☐ Are you irritable a lot?
- ☐ Are you on high alert all the time, watching the addict-alcoholic for signs of using?
- ☐ Do you feel embarrassed about the situation with your addicted loved one?
- ☐ Do you feel tired a lot?
- ☐ Has the addict-alcoholic ever made you feel guilty?
- ☐ Does what your brain tells you conflict with what your gut instinct tells you?

- ☐ Do you find yourself quick to anger sometimes?
- ☐ When you confront the addict-alcoholic, do you ever end up feeling confused and conflicted?
- ☐ Are you not as confident as you used to be?
- ☐ Do you feel alone, like nobody understands what you are going through?
- ☐ Do you frequently try to control situations around you?
- ☐ Do you feel anxious a lot?
- ☐ Do you feel any resentment toward the addict-alcoholic?
- ☐ Is it hard for you to relax?
- ☐ Do you feel like you can't do anything right when it comes to the addict-alcoholic?
- ☐ Are you a perfectionist or an overachiever?
- ☐ Have you ever felt foolish about yourself?
- ☐ Have you ever thought: *Why is this happening to me?*
- ☐ Do you find it hard to allow other people to struggle without trying to rescue them?
- ☐ Do you find it hard to allow yourself to be vulnerable in relationships with people besides the addict-alcoholic?
- ☐ Do you ever feel like things are out of control and it scares you?
- ☐ Do you seem to always have crises or chaos around you?
- ☐ Do you avoid conflict?
- ☐ Do you ever feel inadequate, that no matter what you do it's not good enough?

☐ Have you ever felt betrayed by your addicted loved one?

☐ Do you have a hard time getting a good night's sleep?

If you answered yes to at least a few of the questions above, you are feeling the effects of living with an addict-alcoholic who is manipulating you. You have emotional wounds which need healing!

6.11 THE PROCESS OF HEALING

The process of healing from living with active addiction could be summarized by "discover, uncover, recover":

1. Discover (get the facts)

Educate yourself on the disease of addiction and the mechanics of how addicts manipulate.

2. Uncover (understand the problem)

Learn how living with active addict-alcoholics and their manipulation creates emotional states in you. Then link the internal emotional states to your behavioral tendencies. This shows you how you arrived at the state you are in.

Once you gain an understanding of what has been done to you and how it has affected you, the problem has been defined.

3. Recover (heal)

Now you know what you are healing from, the process of healing may begin.

6.12 SO, HOW CAN YOU SUPPORT THE ADDICT-ALCOHOLIC?

As we discussed, addict-alcoholics will control and manipulate people like you into tolerating their using. The constant manipulation has caused your relationship to become unhealthy. They must keep it that way if they are to persuade you to tolerate their using.

So, how do you support and help your addicted loved one when your relationship has become unhealthy? The first step is to not participate in the unhealthy behaviors or communication. As you probably have discovered in your own relationship with the addict-alcoholic, you cannot control them. All you have control over is yourself. So, the way to be as supportive as possible is to be the heathiest version of yourself you can be. Know that sometimes being the healthiest version of your self means helping them, while other times it means setting healthy boundaries and detaching with love.

Ultimately it is up to the addict-alcoholic to do the things which will help them get better. You can't do that for them.

Remember my metaphor for the person stuck in the well from section 3.17? Don't go into the well with them! When you do the things listed below, you will become the person standing outside the well, lowering the rope, and truly helping them … as well as yourself! Here is one more thing: know that there may be times where there is no rope you can lower that will help, or that you shouldn't be the one lowering the rope. There are instances when it is 100% up to the addict-alcoholic to help themselves.

Here are some ways you can step out of unhealthy behaviors:

1. Get as educated as possible on the disease of addiction.

When you know the facts about the disease of addiction, the addict-alcoholic can't twist facts and control your perception of their addiction.

Reading this book has given you a good start. There are many other great books out there for you to continue to learn. There are some resource recommendations in the "Resources" section at the end of this book.

2. Take care of yourself.

People like you frequently focus on the addict-alcoholic so much they don't take care of themselves. This is how loved ones like you become burnt out, worn down, and exhausted. If you are exhausted, how are you going to help them?

Don't stop doing the things which make you happy. Go to the gym and work out, go out to lunch with friends and laugh, read that book you've been wanting to read, get back to the hobby you used to spend so much time on.

Recharge your emotional batteries. As they say in the safety debriefing when you get on an airplane: "Parents, put your oxygen mask on first before helping your children with theirs."

By reading this book, you are off to a good start!

3. Create healthy boundaries and stop enabling your addict-alcoholic.

Remember this quote I wrote earlier: "What you tolerate, you encourage." When you tolerate sick behavior, you are helping to cultivate a sick relationship.

Beyond the Lies has given a glimpse behind the scenes of what is really going on in your relationship with the addict-alcoholic. With a clear picture and a clear mind, you can decide for yourself what is acceptable behavior and learn how to defend, with love, your behavioral boundaries.

4. Don't allow yourself to be manipulated, and create change through healthy communication.

Learn how to recognize when addicts are gaslighting you, guilt tripping you, lying, twisting words around, or manipulating you in any other way. Develop healthy responses to create change when you spot a manipulation attempt.

Healthy communication includes:

- stating the facts,
- remaining calm and coming from a position of love,
- not allowing them to shift the topic of your discussion,
- sticking to what you believe in and defending your behavioral boundaries.

The diagram in section 6.3 titled "The addict-alcoholic starts to drink heavily and..." is a great example of how healthy boundaries are breached by the addict-alcoholic. In the example, they challenged your boundary by eliciting sympathy with: "It's been a tough week, and I just want to relax." Their persuasion worked when you thought: *I guess it's OK this time*. If you had already read *Beyond the Lies* when the interaction in the diagram happened, you would be able to spot their manipulation attempt and change the outcome from *I guess it's OK this time* to something like this:

You: "I love you but it's not OK when you drink like this."

Them: "It's been a tough week; I just want to relax."

You: "I get it. You certainly have had a tough week. Let me know how I can support you in any way other than watching you drink. Your drinking is still not OK with me."

In the above alternative outcome, you don't fall for their manipulative attempt at eliciting sympathy. You demonstrated you care for them when you validated their feelings and showed support, then you finished by refortifying the boundary you defined in your first comment. You refused, with love, to participate in the manipulation. You will feel better because that is a much healthier way to address the example situation in the diagram than the outcome of, *I guess it's OK this time.*

When you quit participating in the manipulation game, they can't control you. By breaking the cycle of manipulation one incident at a time, you will create change.

5. Go to Al-Anon or Nar-Anon meetings.

I have discussed these groups multiple times in this book. Giving these groups a fair chance to help you boils down to this:

- Be open-minded.
- Identify with the group members; don't compare and look for why you are different.
- Give it a fair chance; go to multiple different meetings (say five or six) before you make a judgment.

6. Go to an *addiction-literate* therapist.

Not all therapists are fluent in addiction. I can't emphasize how important it is to find a therapist who specializes in addiction because they understand the landscape of living with an addict-alcoholic. The analogy I use for this is

"You wouldn't go to a foot doctor for a heart problem, would you?"

I am not disparaging therapists; they all mean well. It's just that when it comes to addiction, unless they have a lot of experience dealing with it (or better yet, specialize in it), it will be hard for them to help because addict-alcoholics are so good at manipulating and controlling the narrative. Like doctors, therapists are only as good as the information being fed to them.

My wife Nicole and I have direct experience with this and it is in our story below.

* * *

Nicole's and my experience with therapists:

"How could you not know he was drinking that much?!"

It was around the year 2005. Nicole and I were having a tough time in our relationship. I was fully into my alcoholic state at that point, so it's no wonder we were having problems. I did my best to keep my drinking out of the spotlight when it came to discussing our relationship problems. We decided to try marriage counseling.

Nicole found a counselor near us who had good ratings, and we started therapy. In our first appointment, it did not take long for Nicole to express her concerns over my drinking. Now the therapist's attention was on me. So, what did I do? I did what I always did. I downplayed my situation and outright lied about how much I was drinking. Here is the kicker: we usually met at the therapist's office on our way home from work, so we had separate cars, and during the appointments while I lied about how much I had been drinking, I sometimes had beer on ice in the car ready for the ride home after.

At the beginning of our appointments, our therapist would sometimes ask me, "How is your drinking doing?" My generic, nonspecific reply was usually, "It's going good." He never probed further on exactly what "going good" meant, dropping the subject and moving on. Through lack of experience with addiction, he was unable to see through my evasive answers. He was very easy to appease, and this cat-and-mouse game went on for more than five years.

Nicole and I did learn better communication skills and worked through a few of the challenges in our relationship, but we never seemed to really get to the bottom of it all. That was because of me, an active addict-alcoholic. I was protecting my ability to drink and smoke pot by lying, feeding the therapist and Nicole misinformation.

Eventually, Nicole started seeing another practitioner in the same office for her own personal therapy. It was during this time of joint and personal counseling sessions that I finally hit my rock bottom, admitted that I was an addict-alcoholic, and got sober.

I finally got honest with Nicole about how much I drank and smoked pot. She told me she knew I was having more than she was seeing, but she had no idea that it was at the level I told her … which was twelve to fifteen beers every day and pot every few hours. She didn't know because I was an expert hider, as many addict-alcoholics are.

The topic of my addiction was obviously front and center for the next several marriage counseling sessions. Our marriage therapist did not act surprised once I revealed I was an addict-alcoholic. Here's the other thing though, in all those years leading up to this moment he never seemed to suspect that addiction could have been playing a big part of our marital problems. Of course, this was because I lied to him all that time.

Soon after that, during one of Nicole's sessions with her personal therapist, she of course talked about all that had transpired with me getting sober and what I had revealed to her about how much I was drinking. Her therapist's response to this was, "How could you not know he was drinking that much?!" Nicole was taken aback. The comment really made her feel stupid for not knowing how much I was drinking. It was then that Nicole realized her therapist lacked experience with addiction. Nicole was not stupid; I was an expert hider, a highly functioning addict-alcoholic, and I was manipulating her.

Both Nicole and I really embraced recovery. Early on I went to recovery meetings almost every day and she went to Al-Anon multiple times a week. We both learned a lot about addiction from those meetings and what it did to our relationship. From that side of our recovery, what we realized is while the therapists were very qualified professionals, truly cared and were trying to help, they just didn't have the expertise to help us. We sought out a marriage counselor who also specialized in addiction, and it turns out he was in recovery himself. We found that experience very helpful, especially since I was in early recovery and prone to heavy mood swings as I reworked my whole toolbox for coping with life.

* * *

Like I said before, you wouldn't go to a foot doctor for a heart problem, now would you? As you can see, the same applies to finding a therapist when addiction is involved. I want to re-emphasize that the therapists we worked with were very good at their profession and truly trying to help us. They just didn't know what they didn't know. I tell you that the second marriage counselor we saw who also specialized in addiction did know. When I got sober, my old manipulation habits didn't instantly disappear, and he was able to see through any kind of truth twisting I did during our sessions. He knew how we addict-alcoholics operated. He would not have allowed me to answer the question "How is your drinking going?" with the evasive, nonspecific response of "It's going good." He also knew the impact Nicole had suffered from living with me all those years. He was very supportive because he knew what our entire household was going through during the time I got sober.

6.13 PLEASE KEEP GOING!

I hope I have validated your experience and given you a greater understanding of how you have been affected by the addict-alcoholic in your life. To support them, you must first come from a healthy place, and it is my goal to help you get there.

Do you want to help your addicted loved one? Do you want to feel better? Did you relate to any of the checklist items in section 6.9, "What effect does manipulation have on you?"

If you answered yes to any of those questions, please keep going. In section 6.11, I laid out the pathway of

1. Discover (get the facts)
2. Uncover (understand the problem)
3. Recover (you need healing too)

There will be more to come from me. In my next book we will dive into more detail regarding uncovering and understanding the problem because it is my belief that if we don't understand the problem in its entirety, then it is impossible to know what the right solution is.

In the meantime, I have listed some resources in the final section for you to check out. When you continue to discover the facts, you will learn more than what the addict-alcoholic themselves know.

Thank you for spending this time with me. Don't forget to keep an eye out for my next book! Remember, put your oxygen mask on first before helping your loved one with theirs.

A letter to my readers, from Craig

I want to thank you for reading *Beyond the Lies.* My goal in writing this book was to get you inside the head of an addict or alcoholic and give a more complete picture of what it means to have an addicted loved one.

If you found this book helpful, I would be grateful if you could leave a review on whichever website you purchased it to help other people discover this resource.

To keep up to date with the latest plans for book signings, new books, interviews, or other engagements, please check out the link below (hint: there will be more books!).

CSJacksonEvolve.com

I also would love to hear from you directly. Please don't hesitate to send me comments on how this was helpful, not helpful, suggestions for additions, or things you may have disagreed with. It's all OK and I want to hear from you! Contact me through my website above.

For more information about my books, follow me on Amazon!

With gratitude,
Craig

Resources for Loved Ones of Addicts and Alcoholics

Support groups and community resources

- **Al-Anon Family Groups: https://al-anon.org**
For families and friends of alcoholics. Offers in-person and virtual meetings, literature, and support communities. Includes Alateen for teenagers.

- **Nar-Anon Family Groups: www.nar-anon.org**
For those affected by someone else's drug use. Offers 12-step meetings and support literature.

- **Families Anonymous: www.familiesanonymous.org**
12-step fellowship for relatives and friends of those with drug, alcohol, or behavioral issues.

- **SMART Recovery Family and Friends: www.smartrecovery.org/family/**
Based on CRAFT principles (Community Reinforcement and Family Training,). Offers tools and meetings to support loved ones constructively.

- **In The Rooms: www.intherooms.com/home/**
A global recovery community offering virtual meetings, including support for family members and friends.

Educational and practical support

• **Partnership to End Addiction: https://drugfree.org/**
Offers a wealth of resources for parents and caregivers, including free coaching, email/text support, and science-based guidance.

• **SAMHSA Family Resources: www.samhsa.gov/families**
U.S. government resource hub for families, with treatment locators and information on substance use and mental health.

• **National Institute on Drug Abuse – For Families: https://nida.nih.gov/research-topics/parents-educators**
Science-based resources for understanding addiction and supporting someone in recovery.

Crisis support and helplines

• **SAMHSA's National Helpline: www.samhsa.gov/find-help/national-helpline**
24/7 confidential treatment referral and information service in English and Spanish. Phone: 1-800-662-HELP (4357)

• **National Alliance on Mental Illness (NAMI): www.nami.org/help**
Support and education for families dealing with co-occurring mental illness and addiction.
Phone: 1-800-950-NAMI (6264)

Other books for families and loved ones

• ***Beyond Addiction*** by Jeffrey Foote, et al.:

www.amazon.com/Beyond-Addiction-Science-Kindness-People/dp/1476709483
Practical, evidence-based guidance for helping someone change.

• ***Codependent No More*** by Melody Beattie:
www.amazon.com/Codependent-No-More-Controlling-Yourself/dp/0894864025
A foundational book for those who struggle with codependency in relationships with addicts.

• ***Addict in the House*** by Robin Barnett:
www.amazon.com/Addict-House-No-Nonsense-Addiction-Recovery/dp/1626252607
A direct, empowering guide for families living with someone in active addiction.